"Jack Hibbs has been a good friend, [...] he Word for nearly three decades. I high[...] he deception that has left the church and the world in dazed confusion. His mission, which he does so well, is to prepare the saints for the soon and imminent return of Christ for His church. Jack's commitment to Scripture is strong, his love for the church is passionate, and his service to the Lord is unceasing."

—**Amir Tsarfati**, founder and president of Behold Israel

"This is the kind of book you would expect from Jack Hibbs: biblical, bold, and prophetic. The book especially stresses the need for discernment in our age of confusion and compromise. It covers a wide range of cultural issues, but always stresses the need to honor God rather than give the woke culture what it wants."

—**Dr. Erwin W. Lutzer**, pastor emeritus, Moody Church, Chicago

"The most dangerous part of being deceived is that you don't know you're being deceived! In *Living in the Daze of Deception*, Pastor Jack Hibbs will undeceive you by opening your eyes to God's truth with the engaging clarity that makes so many (like me) love him. Jack holds nothing back to help you become a better disciple and kingdom builder in a world that seems to grow darker and more deceptive by the day. Get this book now!"

—**Frank Turek**, president, CrossExamined.org; coauthor of *I Don't Have Enough Faith to Be an Atheist*

"George Orwell said that to tell the truth in a time of universal deceit is a revolutionary act. The pressures inflicted by evil to bend a knee can make a reasonable man question his own sense of reality. I've lived it. In a world where nothing seems to make sense anymore, where we're 'living in the daze of deception,' there can be only one truth. My friend Pastor Jack provides clarity on how to tell when evil is disguised as good. As an investigative reporter, I agree with Jack when he says that what's happening in America is subversion. As Jack writes, 'True love is telling it like it is,' and *Living in the Daze of Deception* helps us do that."

—**James O'Keefe**, award-winning journalist; author of the *New York Times* bestseller *Breakthrough*

"Pastor Jack Hibbs's book *Living in the Daze of Deception* accurately and fearlessly describes the bizarre turmoil experienced by people across the globe the past few years. The origin of this unending chaos is a sea of lies based in delusion, insisting that what we're experiencing is normal.

But our times are not normal. *Living in the Daze of Deception* explains the biblical Romans 1 delusions of our day and offers a way forward for anyone who seeks to live with discernment."

—**Hon. Michele Bachmann**, dean, Robertson School of Government, Regent University, VA

"Jack Hibbs provides a timely and profound discussion on the state of the church and God's people. It has become increasingly evident that the modern church has lost its mighty impact and isn't reaching a lost and fallen world. Why? We are too concerned with pursuing happiness and altogether too unconcerned with pursuing God. This book is a must-read for all Christians who want to come out of the daze of deception, suit up in the full armor of God, and truly fulfill the great commission."

—**Jenna Ellis**, attorney and host of *Jenna Ellis in the Morning* on American Family Radio

LIVING IN THE
DAZE
OF DECEPTION

JACK HIBBS

HARVEST HOUSE PUBLISHERS
EUGENE, OREGON

Unless otherwise indicated, all Scripture verses are taken from the New King James Version®. Copyright © 1982 by Thomas Nelson. Used by permission. All rights reserved.

Verses marked KJV are taken from the King James Version of the Bible.

Verses marked NLT are taken from the Holy Bible, New Living Translation, copyright © 1996, 2004, 2015 by Tyndale House Foundation. Used by permission of Tyndale House Publishers, Inc., Carol Stream, Illinois 60188. All rights reserved.

Cover design by Faceout Studio

Cover images © tomertu, Igor Vitkovskiy, Golubovy / Shutterstock

Interior design by Aesthetic Soup

For bulk, special sales, or ministry purchases, please call 1-800-547-8979.
Email: CustomerService@hhpbooks.com

This logo is a federally registered trademark of the Hawkins Children's LLC. Harvest House Publishers, Inc., is the exclusive licensee of this trademark.

Living in the Daze of Deception
Copyright © 2024 by Jack Hibbs
Published by Harvest House Publishers
Eugene, Oregon 97408
www.harvesthousepublishers.com

ISBN 978-0-7369-8738-7 (pbk)
ISBN 978-0-7369-8739-4 (eBook)

Library of Congress Control Number: 2023938672

All rights reserved. No part of this publication may be reproduced, stored in a retrieval system, or transmitted in any form or by any means—electronic, mechanical, digital, photocopy, recording, or any other—except for brief quotations in printed reviews, without the prior permission of the publisher.

Printed in the United States of America

24 25 26 27 28 29 30 31 32 / BP / 10 9 8 7 6 5 4 3 2

This book is dedicated to our children and grandchildren.

To your children and grandchildren,

and to all those who must navigate the future

starting today with truth and courage,

which will see us through the DAZE ahead.

ACKNOWLEDGMENTS

With special thanks to Judi McDaniels, whose tireless efforts
and constant encouragement made this book possible.

To my precious family, who sacrificed their time
so that I could write this book by stealing time away from them.

To my beautiful, steadfast, and faithful wife, Lisa,
who has always been my constant companion and sounding board
throughout 45 years of love and marriage
and this amazing life of ministry.

And to my Jesus Christ, who, when I was in
the valley of the shadow of death, gave me life.

Jack Hibbs
Chino Hills, California

CONTENTS

MIKE POMPEO

S ometimes, simple truths told directly, humbly, and with love can affect lives. Pastor Jack's timely work will do that.

I opened my remarks to the American University of Cairo in Egypt on January 10, 2019, with three simple, declarative sentences: "I'm Mike Pompeo. I'm America's Secretary of State. And I am an evangelical Christian." It's an understatement to say it is rare to hear a United States Secretary of State proclaim his faith in such a setting. My own team strongly opposed me saying it. *The New York Times*, the flagship of the mainstream media, declared my remarks had sparked a "revolt" at the university. But these words were both true and important. They needed to be said so that America's adversaries and allies would know my worldview and how I would approach threats to the American people. The central ideas Pastor Jack details in this book make it clear that we should approach the threats to our souls and our faith with equal directness.

Over the ensuing 1,000 days that I served as America's Secretary of State, I always made it my mission to clearly understand the problem, call it out by name, and develop strategic and concrete approaches to fixing it. From China to North Korea to Iran and so many others, we took the same approach: Be honest about the problem with yourself and the American people, and work hard to find a solution. Too often, Washington politicians tiptoe around issues, afraid to offend someone or some group. But solving a problem always begins with understanding reality. In this book, Pastor Jack uses the same approach to provide Christians with a clear view of the world and how we must respond.

Today, America faces no greater external, earthly threat than the Chinese Communist Party, an atheistic governing body that seeks total subservience from its own people and total deference from other nations. I saw it up close and personal as Secretary of State: This regime has no respect for human rights because it has no respect for human life; indeed, the only thing that matters to the CCP is the continuation of its power. China absolutely seeks to remake the world so that its model of tyranny can prosper. The CCP wants humanity to live in their fog, their daze. Pastor Jack correctly points us toward the deception of our adversaries, via propaganda, and the deception of our leaders by controlling the flow of information so they can advance their agendas. The consequences of such tyranny for Christians—indeed, for all of humanity—can be truly terrible and wicked.

If the United States is to face down its challenges—as it did with Communist Russia—we will need the moral witness of Christianity. We will need a strong, vibrant church that is prepared to remind Americans of the foundations of our freedom, which undoubtedly flow from the Judeo-Christian understanding that we are all created in God's image and are therefore endowed with "certain inalienable rights."

Yet Western nations—originally the defenders of the Christian faith—are working to remove faith from their societies entirely, something Pastor Jack describes in detail in the pages ahead. Today, we are told to place our faith not in God, but in grievance, victimhood, and tribalism.

We are told there is no such thing as God, truth, or good and evil. The true threat to America and all free people lies in this ideology.

Pastor Jack gets it exactly right: If we lose our faith as a nation, we will not survive. We will lack the courage and certainty necessary to confront the CCP, and we will crumble from within.

As this book makes clear, though, now is not the time to despair. Evil is a fact of life, and it always has been. Rather than appease or compromise, we must meet evil today in the same manner as the apostle Paul instructed the church in Ephesus: "Put on the whole armor of God, that you may be able to stand against the schemes of the devil."

In *Living in the Daze of Deception*, Pastor Jack outlines for all believers how we can do this: by faithfully trusting in Jesus, proclaiming Him as our Savior, and following Scripture.

Without Christ, I know that I would be lost. My walk with Him began many years ago at the United States Military Academy at West Point after I was invited to a Bible study led by two upper-class cadets. Though much in the world has changed since then, my faith has remained an indispensable light and my surest support: Through my service in the military, running two small businesses, serving in Congress, and dealing with the challenges facing America as CIA Director and Secretary of State, I have been able to persevere only through God's grace.

If we have faith, God will work in surprising and wonderful ways to continually prepare us to meet the challenges ahead. I know I would have never possessed the courage to proclaim my faith in Cairo had I not first been blessed years before with the chance to share it with a room full of precocious, rowdy fifth graders while teaching a Sunday school session with my wife, Susan, at Eastminster Presbyterian in Wichita, Kansas. This proved doubly beneficial too: My role often encompassed keeping the boys in their seats—this was the best preparation for a career in international diplomacy!

I share Pastor Jack's faith and optimism. Jesus Christ overcame our sin and all sin, forever. He overcame death. Through Him, I know we can overcome the wickedness we face today.

Be unapologetic; be unyielding. Always approach, in love, those who persecute you. Christ can truly change hearts, and it is for this reason that I know you will find this book as encouraging as I did.

God bless you, and always keep your faith.

—Mike Pompeo

PART 1

RECOGNIZING THE MANY KINDS OF DECEPTION

CHAPTER 1

THE DAZE OF GLOBAL DECEPTION

Viewed from NASA's Terra satellite, it gives the impression of a massive meadow of snow or a vast glacier—calm, serene, and mesmerizing. But locals descending the steep, twisting section of Interstate 5 from California's Tehachapi Mountains know better. They understand they are entering the Central Valley's hazardous tule fog and that they should drive with caution. When conditions are right, the thick fog causes unsuspecting drivers to lose their sense of direction with tragic, sometimes deadly consequences. In November 2007, tule fog caused a 108-car pileup resulting in two deaths and almost 40 injuries. The pileup, which included 18 semitrailer trucks, extended for nearly a mile and closed CA-99 for more than 12 hours. The last vehicle collided ten minutes after the initial crash.[1]

In today's world, fog, tule or otherwise, characterizes the disorienting daze in which we have entered and now live. Hence the title of this book and the reason why I intentionally substituted the word *daze* in place of *days*.

Usually, when the word *days* is mentioned, most people understand it to concern a particular time or a period. Certainly, this book deals with a specific time that the Bible says will visit humanity—a time of unparalleled difficulty such as the world has never seen. But my primary focus is to help you identify the daze of deception enveloping us today.

Deception, like fog, acts as camouflage—blurring and concealing what is right in front of us. Safely navigating it requires us to use the same precautions drivers use—take heed of flashing lights or warning signals ahead and keep an eye out for patches of clear sky, or in this case, biblical truth, to act as a guide.

Various dictionaries define *daze* as the inability to think or react properly, to be bewildered or numbed. Synonyms include *stupefy, shock, confound,* and *distract.* I believe each of these words can be applied to people's reactions to the all-encompassing sinister changes taking place today. More than any time in recent memory, people are demonstrating an extraordinary lack of judgment and the inability to think or act appropriately when it comes to what they believe and how they live. How is this happening? Why like never before in history?

What you are about to read on the following pages is an outline of the many ways deception is influencing our world—and, more importantly, how we as followers of Jesus can equip ourselves to respond effectively to it. My prayer is that you will understand how the strong hand of God Himself will steer you through an otherwise dazed and confused world with hope, clarity, and direction from above.

CAUGHT OFF GUARD

Deception has become so widespread that it affects all of us today. Here is just one example of what I'm talking about: Have you noticed the incredible amount of deceptive misinformation, false reporting, and, as has been popularly called, fake news that has spread through the media these last several years? The answer is yes, of course. All of us who utilize television news, the internet, and social media will readily agree because so much of what is said runs contrary to what we know to be factual. Yet there are other times when we can't be sure of what's true. Even when a person raises their right hand and swears under oath in a court of law, we're still not always sure whether they are telling the absolute truth. Discovering the truth has become an almost impossible task, leaving us wondering what to believe.

You have probably heard the classic tale of what transpired in the ancient city of Troy when the Greeks constructed an enormous wooden horse, gifted it to their enemy, and pretended to sail away. Their Trojan enemies pulled the horse into the city without realizing that hidden within were Greek soldiers who would sneak out and unlock the city gates from inside so that the supposedly departed Greek army could return and attack. The outcome was that Troy was overtaken and destroyed.

The Trojan horse eventually came to symbolize a deceptive trick or strategy employed when there seemed to be no way to defeat a powerful enemy. Today, you would shake your head if you saw a 25-foot-tall wooden horse roll into your city. But have you thought about what is being concealed by powerful elites, organizations, and governing authorities, or the unexplainable level of secrecy tied to their deceptive views? When you realize that these people and groups often consider you their enemy, the reality of modern-day Trojan horses doesn't seem beyond the realm of possibility. It is also important to understand that wicked schemes come in small packages too—subtly hidden in an element of truth—making them more dangerous and difficult to spot.

I believe that what makes the most recent decade unique is the extent to which misleading information has permeated not only our culture in the West but also globally. An outstanding example is what happened in the wake of the COVID pandemic. No matter what your view or position or the pain and sorrow suffered during the pandemic, one thing is certain: The "experts" and political powerbrokers, along with biotechnology corporations, learned that by controlling the flow of information, they could rapidly advance their agendas.

Quickly following on the heels of the pandemic was a worldwide outbreak of irrational and even unstable thinking when it came to things like gender identity, marriage, the sanctity of life, and the rule of law. Closer to home, there were questions about national borders and whether America should keep its Constitution. So many things were brought into question, and even more are being challenged today.

What does all this mean? First, deception is continually at work through the conversations, thoughts, and actions of those who reject the very concept of God from their belief systems. I know that sounds brutal, but that's backed by what the Bible says. And second, we must be careful not to dismiss deception as taking place only in the media or the social and political realms. Jesus warned that there would be tremendous spiritual deception in the last days before His physical return to Earth.

THE DAZE OF THE LAST DAYS
What Are the Last Days?

Over the years, I have been asked by many news outlets and genuinely concerned seekers alike, "What are the last days?" I think it is awesome that whenever there is a significant world crisis, the church's phones ring nonstop because people want to know what is happening. The callers on the other end ask, "Could it be that the beginning of the end is near?" or, "Is Armageddon right around the corner?" The world wants answers when things begin to shake both literally and figuratively.

Let me share a scripture that applies to every Christ-follower in the last days: "Sanctify the Lord God in your hearts, and always be ready to give a defense to everyone who asks you a reason for the hope that is in you, with meekness and fear" (1 Peter 3:15).

Here, and in other verses, it is clearly stated that God's people need to be ready and able to give the answers that nonbelievers are seeking. That means it is incumbent that Christians know and understand what they believe and how that knowledge plays out in everyday life.

When we talk about the last days, you need to know that throughout the Bible, the concept of *last days* appears in a variety of ways: the end of times, the end of days, the last day, the latter times, the end of the age, or, as 1 John 2:18 puts it, the last hour. Not all those terms speak about the exact same thing, but all of them refer to the conclusion of things, which includes the return of Jesus Christ and the establishment of His kingdom here on Earth.

The events we collectively call the last days are all part of what is called Bible prophecy or biblical eschatology. Bible prophecy is God writing the future in advance so that we can know what lies ahead. Many churches shy away from teaching prophecy out of biblical ignorance, because of the denomination they affiliate with, or because they think it's going to generate fear. Whatever the reason, the refusal to teach prophecy is a shame. The Bible reveals details about the last days to alleviate the stress of wondering what is coming and to prepare us so that we will be ready.

Because we should be familiar with our Bibles, God expects us to know what His Word says about future events. Throughout the ministry of Jesus, the religious leaders continually attacked Him regarding His doctrine of salvation, His doctrine of faith, and interestingly, His doctrine concerning the last days. In Matthew 16:1, the Pharisees and Sadducees came to Jesus, asking that He show them a sign from heaven. Here is what He said:

> When it is evening you say, "It will be fair weather, for the sky is red"; and in the morning, "It will be foul weather today, for the sky is red and threatening." Hypocrites! You know how to discern the face of the sky, but you cannot discern the signs of the times (Matthew 16:2-3).

I love how subtle Jesus is. You hypocrites! You can forecast the weather but can't discern the times and signs of the last days. May that never be said of you or me.

What Are the Signs of the Last Days?

Detailed volumes have been written about the signs of the end of the age, and we should understand these signs. By giving you just a few indicators of what will happen during the last days, I believe I can make my point that this is the time in which you and I live.

Scripture says that men would be haters of God, lovers of pleasure, lovers of lust and evil, and lovers of the things of this world while, at the same time, becoming loveless and uncaring toward the general population and the welfare of their fellow man (2 Timothy 3:2-4).

No one can deny that each of these behaviors is now commonplace. But I ask you: By what standard are we to judge that any of the behaviors I just mentioned are wrong? Do you make that judgment call? Do I? Or do we allow popular opinion or government agencies to decide for us? The only reason any of these questions arise is that God is nowhere present in the hearts and minds of people. Practically speaking, they are haters of God. Think about it. If there's no God, then there are no rules. And when there are no rules, there is lawlessness. And when there's lawlessness, there's nothing left but me, myself, and what I want, and then everything becomes acceptable for me.

We also know that before Christ returns, demonic doctrines will flood our world, resulting in a widespread apostasy or departure from faith in God. Now, don't get the idea this means there are some strange, fuzzy creatures lurking around in the shadows, trying to trick people. If that were true, they would be easy to identify. What is true is that demonic powers have commandeered church pulpits and corrupted the gospel's message, weakening or wiping out the faith of those sitting in the pews—just as Scripture warns.

> The Spirit expressly says that in latter times some will depart from the faith, giving heed to deceiving spirits and doctrines of demons (1 Timothy 4:1).

> The time will come when they will not endure sound doctrine, but according to their own desires, because they have itching ears, they will heap up for themselves teachers; and

they will turn their ears away from the truth, and be turned aside to fables (2 Timothy 4:3-4).

God's Word has gone missing in many houses of worship today. Ministries are preaching messages of self-centeredness, prosperity, and me-ism versus sound doctrine. Can you see how this disconnect has allowed Christ-followers to be confused by the daze of deception? This is why we see believers who cannot distinguish right from wrong and have departed from biblical orthodoxy while embracing a secular form of Christianity.

How, then, can we inoculate ourselves against deception? How can we know the truth? In some instances, we may never know the truth when it comes to politics, some military scheme or venture, or a business deal gone wrong. But when it comes to spiritual realities, there's only one way to know the truth. That, of course, is the Bible—the inerrant, perfect, never-changing Word of God. When the church—the ground and pillar of all truth—proclaims the whole counsel of God from the Bible, deception will not and cannot take hold.

THE EVENTS OF THE LAST DAYS HAVE BEEN DESIGNED
...to Validate God

The global crises of our day—the saber-rattlings of war, the lack of trustworthy leaders, the potential collapse of national economies, the controversies over cryptocurrencies, and the government overreach during health pandemics—may not make sense to you and me. But rest assured, they do to God. What do I mean by that? Isaiah 46:9-10 says,

> Remember the former things of old, for I am God, and there is no other; I am God, and there is none like Me, declaring the end from the beginning, and from ancient times things that are not yet done, saying, "My counsel shall stand, and I will do all My pleasure."

Isaiah 45:21-22 elaborates further on this same truth:

> Tell and bring forth your case; yes, let them take counsel
> together. Who has declared this from ancient time? Who has
> told it from that time? Have not I, the LORD? And there is
> no other God besides Me, a just God and a Savior; there is
> none besides Me. "Look to Me, and be saved, all you ends
> of the earth! For I am God, and there is no other."

Only God knows the future, my friend. And the fact that the God
of the Bible tells us what is going to happen before it comes to pass validates that He exists, He alone is God, and He will accomplish all that
He desires.

Are you perplexed? Are you looking for answers? Turn off your TV,
close your laptop, set down your phone, and pick up the Bible. I have
lost track of how many times I have had a conversation that goes something like this:

"Pastor, how can I know if God is real?"

"Open the book, read it, and watch what happens."

"But isn't that brainwashing?"

"Absolutely!"

In this dirty, messed-up world, you and I need a good brainwashing—we need to let the Bible get inside and scrub away all the gunk
accumulated throughout the day, let alone a lifetime. God's Word cleanses
and straightens out our thinking. Whether you're uncertain if God is
real or if He is trustworthy, I promise those assurances will come through
His Word.

Today you should ask yourself, "What did the God of antiquity do?
And how did it relate to what He said in advance that He would do?" If
you take a careful look at the historical proofs regarding what the Bible
says in answer to those questions, you will realize that you can trust God
with every detail of your life.

...to Validate the Bible

If you question whether God exists, you probably have doubts about the Bible too. Doubts like, *Are the Bible's claims accurate? Can I rely upon it for life's answers both now and in the future?* The answer is a resounding yes, and yes! But don't take my word for it. Second Peter 1:19 tells why you can trust in the fulfillment of every part of God's Word: "We have the prophetic word confirmed, which you do well to heed as a light that shines in a dark place."

The King James Version translates "prophetic word confirmed" as "a more sure word of prophecy," which, in the Greek language, means "firm, faithful, permanent, or morally true and certain.", God's past performance in fulfilling written prophecy

> The fact that the God of the Bible tells us what is going to happen before it comes to pass validates that He exists, He alone is God, and He will accomplish all that He desires.

settles the question as to whether He can and will fulfill what He has promised to you now and in the future. To back that up, I need to give you only one word: *Israel*.

To those who were alive in 1947 or before, Israel was ancient history. It didn't appear on a modern map. But for prophecy to be fulfilled, Israel had to become a nation again, and on May 14, 1948, it did just that. After 2,000 years of the Jewish people being in exile, Israel came to life again! It was literally born in one day, just as the Bible said it would be (Isaiah 66:8; Ezekiel 37:12-13). In all of history, no other nation has been a nation, lost its status as a nation, and then been reinstated as a nation.

No other book or person can make the accurate prophetic claims that the Bible does. *The History Channel* and others will often cite purported prophets like Nostradamus, who had a dismal record of being right in his predictions. Biblical prophets had no such leeway—they had to be

100 percent accurate. This is how you can tell the difference between God's prophets and false prophets.

Are you sensing the world's darkness creeping in and slowly causing you to feel a bit foggy, even dazed? You can rely on the "sure word" of the Old Testament prophecies, which 2 Peter 1:19 compares to "a light that shines in a dark place." Are there circumstances beyond your control pressing against you? Flee to the Word! Psalm 119:105 says, "Your word is a lamp to my feet and a light to my path."

> God's Word inspires confidence that translates into hope and moves us beyond merely surviving to thriving.

Scripture doesn't give us some esoteric mystery that we need to contemplate while sitting on a rock. It provides us with the wisdom and understanding we need to navigate our way through life. Understanding how biblical prophecy is unfolding will increase your confidence in the Bible as a whole. God's Word inspires confidence that translates into hope and moves us beyond merely surviving to thriving.

...to Validate Jesus Christ

From the moment He entered this world, Jesus Christ has been under attack. He was mocked and ridiculed, destined to become a common curse word. I mean, watch someone slam a door on their finger and listen to what comes out of their mouth. I've never heard anyone say, "Oh, Buddha!" or "Oh, Mohammed, that really hurts!" But they have no problem inserting Jesus' name in that kind of exclamation.

I find it significant that only one person in all of history has drawn such universal attention, ire, and hatred. But it's to be expected because Satan hates Christ. He will do anything and everything he can to neutralize the Son of God. What is awesome about the unfolding of prophetic events is that they validate the reality of who Jesus is.

Jesus never hid the fact that He would be crucified, and He knew that even His disciples would doubt He was the Son of God when it happened. This is what made His words to them so vital to their faith. "Now I tell you before it comes, that when it does come to pass, you may believe that *I am He*" (John 13:19). Notice the phrase "I am He." Jesus was saying, "I am telling you things before they happen so that when they do, you will know that I AM." To the Jewish ear, that was one bold statement!

The announcement "I AM" is the same one made by God to Moses on Mount Sinai. God commissioned Moses to go to the children of Israel with a message of freedom, but Moses wanted details. He asked God, "Who do I tell them sent me?" God answered him, saying, "'I AM WHO I AM.' And He said, 'Thus you shall say to the children of Israel, "I AM has sent me to you"'" (Exodus 3:14).

What does "I AM WHO I AM" mean? Was God trying to avoid giving Moses His name? On the contrary, God went far beyond merely stating His name. He revealed an essential component of His character to Moses. He was letting Moses know that the eternally present, self-existing God will be there in every situation and circumstance. The New Testament attaches that same theology to Jesus. All the names and attributes of God given in the Old Testament are given to Jesus Christ in the New Testament. We see this in Revelation 1:8: "'I am the Alpha and the Omega, the Beginning and the End,' says the Lord, 'who is and who was and who is to come, the Almighty.'" The Alpha and Omega, the Beginning and the End, refer to God, but Jesus is the one "who is, who was, and is yet to come." Add the statement that Jesus is "the Almighty," and you cannot escape the fact that Jesus and God are one. The God who said, "I will be with you in every situation" is the same God who sent His only Son to provide salvation and eternal life (see John 10:28-29; John 3:16). What comfort. What joy. What a God and Savior!

As the days grow darker and our world races to its conclusion, the prophetic events of the last days indisputably validate Jesus as the soon and coming King. "Worship God! For the testimony of Jesus is the spirit of prophecy" (Revelation 19:10).

...to Validate the Messiah's Identity

As tough as the events of the last days may be, they are meant to give us understanding. In Daniel 12:4, an angel tells Daniel, "You, Daniel, shut up the words, and seal the book until the time of the end; many shall run to and fro, and knowledge shall increase." When you read this verse in the original Hebrew language, it implies that last days' events will cause a turning of a key or will cause a door to open. It was as if the angel said, "Something is going to happen, but until then, Daniel, seal up the book. All you've been shown isn't for now, so don't worry about it."

Most scholars believe, and I agree, that the word "many" refers to the Jewish people in the latter days. They will anxiously run to and fro through the Bible seeking God's purposes. I believe that they are going to look to what has been revealed through the prophets. Daniel says that knowledge will increase, and some people have said, "Well, that's the explosion of technology. Daniel was prophesying the rapid growth of technology." There certainly has been an explosion of technological knowledge, but the announcement given in Daniel was to God's people, His city, and the nation of Israel, *for the future*. I believe a time will come when Israel pursues and hunts and searches the Word of God for a clearer understanding of the prophets and their words regarding the Messiah.

What about you? Have you searched prophetic scriptures for understanding? Do you know where in Scripture Jesus' birthplace was foretold—written some 500 years before His physical birth?

> You, Bethlehem Ephrathah,
> though you are little among the thousands of Judah,
> yet out of you shall come forth to Me
> the One to be Ruler in Israel,
> whose goings forth are from of old,
> from everlasting (Micah 5:2).

And its fulfillment?

> When he had gathered all the chief priests and scribes of
> the people together, he inquired of them where the Christ
> was to be born.
> So they said to him, "In Bethlehem of Judea, for thus it is
> written by the prophet:
>> 'But you, Bethlehem, in the land of Judah,
>> are not the least among the rulers of Judah;
>> for out of you shall come a Ruler
>> who will shepherd My people Israel'" (Matthew 2:4-6).

How about the prophecy that in death, Jesus the Messiah would
become the perfect sacrifice?

> Sacrifice and offering You did not desire;
> my ears You have opened.
> Burnt offering and sin offering You did not require.
> Then I said, "Behold, I come;
> in the scroll of the book it is written of me.
> I delight to do Your will, O my God,
> and Your law is within my heart" (Psalm 40:6-8).

And its fulfillment?

> When He came into the world, He said:
> "Sacrifice and offering You did not desire,
> but a body You have prepared for Me.
> In burnt offerings and sacrifices for sin
> You had no pleasure.
> Then I said, 'Behold, I have come—
> in the volume of the book it is written of Me—
> to do Your will, O God.'"
>
> Previously saying, "Sacrifice and offering, burnt offerings,
> and offerings for sin You did not desire, nor had pleasure in

them" (which are offered according to the law), then He said, "Behold, I have come…to do Your will, O God." He takes away the first that He may establish the second. By that will we have been sanctified through the offering of the body of Jesus Christ once for all (Hebrews 10:5-10).

I don't know about you, but I can't think of anyone else who has ever had his birthplace and manner of death—something that no one can exercise any control over—accurately predicted and fulfilled. The mathematical odds alone are astronomical, if not impossible.

Since prophecy validates Jesus as the Messiah, why should we continue seeking Him until He returns? There are many reasons, but John 1:1-4, 14 offers a powerful one.

In the beginning was the Word, and the Word was with God, and the Word was God. He was in the beginning with God. All things were made through Him, and without Him nothing was made that was made. In Him was life, and the life was the light of men… And the Word became flesh and dwelt among us, and we beheld His glory, the glory as of the only begotten of the Father, full of grace and truth.

I don't mean to sound mystical, but if I understand John correctly, when we read the Scriptures—the Word—from cover to cover, we are looking into the face of God. We are looking at the manifestation of Jesus' life, ministry, and heart in printed form. Even if you are a doubter, that does not take away from the fact that Jesus Christ, the Messiah and Savior of the world, is the physical manifestation of the Word of God (John 1:1).

…to Get Our Attention

Are you uneasy about what the future holds? That is a legitimate concern. It seems as if nearly everything has become unpredictable. Jesus said in Luke 21:26 that men's hearts will fail them "from fear and the expectation of those things which are coming on the earth."

I am not trying to sound alarmist, but what will happen when governments and world economies collapse? What is going to happen when people can't find work, and when they do, inflation and shortages have eaten away their ability to get food for their children? Living in a million-dollar home or driving an expensive car will not matter if you are hungry. We live in a plastic credit-oriented society, built literally out of cards. James 5:2-3 foresaw this type of predicament:

> Your riches are corrupted, and your garments are moth-eaten. Your gold and silver are corroded, and their corrosion will be a witness against you and will eat your flesh like fire. You have heaped up treasure in the last days.

These types of wake-up calls are all around us—each designed to grab our attention. I believe that we need to examine ourselves in this and so many other areas. What, if any, changes do we need to make regarding our commitment to Christ? We can no longer afford to be spectator Christians. Those days are over. Now is the time to be hot-hearted for God, fervently loving the brethren, and living out the Word.

> Let us hold fast the confession of our hope without wavering, for He who promised is faithful. And let us consider one another in order to stir up love and good works, not forsaking the assembling of ourselves together, as is the manner of some, but exhorting one another, and so much the more as you see the Day approaching (Hebrews 10:23-25).

WHY SHOULD YOU CARE?

When you hear messages taught on the last days, it might be tempting to adopt an attitude that says, "They don't apply to me because I'm saved. I won't be here after the rapture to see what happens during the tribulation." Please don't let that kind of thinking take hold, and let me explain why.

There is a Scripture passage concerning the last days that I have not mentioned yet, but I want to give it to you here—Matthew 24:4-8. When questioned about the sign of His coming and the end of the age, Jesus told His disciples,

> Take heed that no one deceives you. For many will come in My name, saying, "I am the Christ," and will deceive many. And you will hear of wars and rumors of wars. See that you are not troubled; for all these things must come to pass, but the end is not yet. For nation will rise against nation, and kingdom against kingdom. And there will be famines, pestilences, and earthquakes in various places. All these are the beginning of sorrows.

Deception, nations at war, drought-producing famines, kingdoms against kingdoms (in the original Greek language, *ethnos* means "ethnic," so this refers to blacks and browns against whites, and reds against yellow, and vice versa), pandemics, and earthquakes—Jesus' words sound like today's news report. Why do I bring this up? Because in the middle of all that calamity and sorrow, Jesus said, "See that you are not troubled." You might assume that I'm suggesting you put on a happy face and think positive thoughts, and everything will be fine. Not so. I appreciate how the late Dr. Ed Hindson put the difficulty of prophetic events into perspective when he said,

> Bible prophecy is not given to us to scare us but to prepare us.
> It is not given to us to frighten us but to invite us.

What great words of encouragement! But is prophecy able to extend such an invitation? Yes, it can. Like Dr. Hindson, I believe that prophecy in Scripture prepares us with the perfect invitation.

Jesus said, "These things [prophecy given in advance] I have spoken to you, that in Me you may have peace. In the world you will have tribulation; but be of good cheer, I have overcome the world" (John 16:33). Jesus overcame sin, death, and hell itself to spare you from the wrath of God Almighty. The promise of heaven and eternal life awaits. You need to hang on to that, and so do the people around you.

Like you, your neighbors, friends, and co-workers are watching the world come unhinged as prophecy unfurls, and they are probably scared. You have to wonder: *Where do they go when things get rough, and they don't have anywhere or anyone to turn to?* Is it Prozac? Smirnoff and Jack Daniels? Entertainment? If that were all I had to hold me up, I'd be worried too.

You can use the last days' events as a catalyst to introduce yourself to neighbors you haven't met yet. Knock on their door and say, "Listen, you may think I'm a lunatic, but I want you to know that I'm a Christ-follower. And with all that is going on right now, I am praying for the neighbors on our street. Do you have any prayer requests?" It is doubtful they will throw you off their porch and slam the door in your face. They'll probably say, "Yeah, you know what? Layoffs are coming at my company. We don't have any savings. Can you pray that I'll keep my job so that I can take care of my family?" Seize that moment! Pray a short prayer, say amen, and promise to keep praying.

In these days of deception, we must seek God-given opportunities to share the truth and love of Jesus Christ. Let's not allow any open door, literally or figuratively, to go to waste.

CHAPTER 2

DAZED BY SPIRITUAL DECEIVERS

H ow often have you heard people yearn for the good old days that they think were somehow simpler and easier than now? I believe that Christians stumble into the same trap when they wish, "If only we lived back in New Testament days." But the truth is, those days weren't easier. First-century Christians endured persecution from the outside and the threat of false teaching on the inside. To be a believer required watchfulness. That is true today as well, which brings us to a very serious and critical topic: identifying a false prophet or false teacher. This is an uncomfortable subject that generally results in negative church growth when preached from the pulpit, but I hope you will stick with me—it's that important to your spiritual growth and maybe even your eternal destination.

In Ecclesiastes 1:9-10, Solomon made an interesting observation that is relevant to our day: "That which has been is what will be, that which is done is what will be done, and there is nothing new under the sun. Is there anything of which it may be said, 'See, this is new'? It has already been in ancient times before us."

Solomon's statement regarding things in the past that will happen again in the future reminds me of watching the New Year's Day Rose Parade. Your view of the parade depends on where you are seated—the beginning, middle, or end. It dictates when you'll see the grand marshal, USC marching band, and spectacular floats. For those lucky enough to be in one of the helicopters high overhead or the Goodyear blimp, you'll get a bird's-eye view of the entire parade—from beginning to end—all at once.

In a similar way, when we look at the entirety of Scripture, we get a panoramic view of the challenges of the past deceptions, the ones happening now, and those that the Bible says are yet future. When it comes to deceivers, we must be on the lookout because "there is nothing new under the sun."

DECEIVERS ARE AMONG US

Jesus warned that as the end of time approaches, deception would increase. So, it makes sense that we can expect slick and persuasive deceivers to emerge from every sector of society. Pundits, professors, politicians, and even corporations are using every opportunity to exert their influence over you. Every time you jump on social media, turn on the television, open a book, or listen to a podcast, someone is there waiting, ready to sway your thinking. Two big questions come to mind: Who is grabbing your attention? Who are you allowing to influence you?

You have got to be wise and discerning about who you follow because—listen carefully—the corporate world, educational institutions, and the media aren't the only domains of deceivers. You will also find them in pulpits and ministries. Oh, they might be incredible speakers—intelligent, funny, and charismatic—but they are bent on leading you down a path of destruction. Heretical teaching has stormed once-healthy churches and cut across denominational lines. Even scarier is the fact that you don't have to leave your house to become their prey.

There are great pastors and skilled teachers on radio, television, and the internet, but not everyone out there is someone worth listening to—and I know Jesus would agree. When you think about Jesus, you might tend to think of the meek and mild Sunday school version of Him, but when He denounced false prophets, the word that comes to my mind is *ballistic*!

Jesus warned,

> Not everyone who says to Me, "Lord, Lord," shall enter the kingdom of heaven, but he who does the will of My Father in heaven. Many will say to Me in that day, "Lord, Lord, have we not prophesied in Your name, cast out demons in Your name, and done many wonders in Your name?" And then I will declare to them, "I never knew you; depart from Me, you who practice lawlessness" (Matthew 7:21-23).

Can you imagine the justifying that these wicked deceivers will have to do when they stand before Jesus on the day of judgment?

"Lord, haven't I prophesied in Your name?"

"Yes, but I wasn't talking to you. I never would have told you to say those things."

"How about the demons I cast out? And don't forget all those great things I did in Your name! People loved it when I came to town."

Imposters can attach Jesus' name to their ministries, but in the end, Jesus will have no choice but to say, "Depart from Me. I never knew you!"

Jesus issued the same condemnation to the hyper-religious scribes and Pharisees when He said, "Woe to you" (Matthew 23:23), which literally means, "Damned be you." Among other things, Jesus rebuked them for being "like whitewashed tombs which indeed appear beautiful outwardly, but inside are full of dead men's bones and all uncleanness. Even so you also outwardly appear righteous to men" (verses 27-28).

These two passages make it plain that even in religious circles, appearances can be misleading. If you want to know the truth about deceivers, you need to look below the surface.

YOU WILL KNOW THEM BY THEIR FRUIT

Don't think false teachers and prophets will cruise into church dressed in a way that identifies them as a foe. If that were true, the ushers would throw them out before they could sit down. According to Jesus, many will look harmless enough, but they want to eat you alive:

> Beware of false prophets, who come to you in sheep's clothing, but inwardly they are ravenous wolves. You will know them by their fruits. Do men gather grapes from thornbushes or figs from thistles? Even so, every good tree bears good fruit, but a bad tree bears bad fruit. A good tree cannot bear bad fruit, nor can a bad tree bear good fruit. Every tree that does not bear good fruit is cut down and thrown into the fire. Therefore by their fruits you will know them (Matthew 7:15-20).

It shouldn't surprise us that false teachers and prophets bear bad fruit. They can't help it—it's their nature. God's law, both in nature and the supernatural realm, is that when you plant corn, up comes corn, not sunflowers. Whatever a man sows, he is going to reap because like seed that goes into the ground, what he has sown is going to germinate, sprout, and then grow until it becomes his reality.

There are many passages in the Bible that describe false teachers and prophets, but 2 Peter 2:10 and 2 Timothy 3:1-5 are great places to start when we're looking at the kinds of fruit these people produce.

In 2 Peter 2:1-22, the apostle Peter had a lot to say about false teachers. I know that Bible translators broke God's Word down into chapters and verses, but in the original Greek text, this passage was one of the longest paragraphs in Scripture. It is as if once Peter got started, he didn't want to stop. I wish I had the space to cover all 22 verses—the passage is so rich—but I want to focus on verse 10, where we read about "those who walk according to the flesh in the lust of uncleanness and despise authority. They are presumptuous, self-willed."

Uncleanness

The danger of false teachers is that they have no problem living according to their own desires, starting with uncleanness. The English word *uncleanness* sounds like something dirty or undesirable, but it is a bit more colorful in Koine Greek. It means "defilement, filth, decay, and rot." Listen, that is bad enough, but now imagine a pit where moisture has collected on the walls. You can smell a grotesque stench, and bugs hover over dead, bloated animals floating in thick muck.

Am I making this too gross for you? Not even close—I can't do the original Greek text justice. My imagination is not vivid enough.

The Bible is incredibly graphic when it describes the wretchedness of these men and women. Sadly, they understand what they are doing, and they'll twist scriptural teachings like "Where sin abounds, grace does much more abound" (see Romans 5:20) to justify their drug abuse, alcoholism, or sexual escapades.

Presumptuous, Self-Willed, and Defiant

Along with being unclean, false teachers are presumptuous (prideful) and self-willed (self-sufficient). It is hard to believe that they could claim to be ministers of Christ and live a life devoted to self. I would say it's an oxymoron. But then again, sin always overplays its hand. It has no self-control. Give it an inch, and it will take a mile. False teachers willingly set themselves above all authority, even God's, in their quest for self-gratification and aggrandizement.

YOU WILL KNOW THEM BY WHAT THEY LOVE

When you read a Scripture passage, it is a good idea to look for repeated words or phrases. Doing so will help you grasp key ideas that the writer is communicating. I point this out because the Holy Spirit is drawing our attention in the passage below to something indicative of false teachers. The word "lovers" is mentioned four times in five verses.

When the wise and aged Paul wrote to Timothy, he warned the young pastor that false teachers would be lovers of self, money, and pleasure, but not of God.

> Know this, that in the last days perilous times will come: For men will be lovers of themselves, lovers of money, boasters, proud, blasphemers, disobedient to parents, unthankful, unholy, unloving, unforgiving, slanderers, without self-control, brutal, despisers of good, traitors, headstrong, haughty, lovers of pleasure rather than lovers of God, having a form of godliness but denying its power. And from such people turn away! (2 Timothy 3:1-5).

Lovers of Self

One characteristic I always see in people who love themselves is ambition. They are out to build their kingdom rather than God's. They love to be the center of attention, and you'll find them up front in some way—feeding off admiring faces pointed their way. The affirmation of others gives them a sense of influence and superiority. But when they can't maneuver into a position of authority, they'll undermine the existing leadership. They will grumble and complain about how others are doing or not doing ministry while promoting themselves and their ideas (Jude 16). Once they realize their tactics aren't working, they'll move on, going from church to church until they get the results they want.

> Sin always overplays its hand. It has no self-control. Give it an inch, and it will take a mile.

It's true that we're all guilty of grumbling and complaining from time to time. When we catch ourselves, we must repent because negative attitudes and words dishonor God. The difference here is that the self-centered grumbler spews out the evil in his heart as a habitual practice.

They don't care if they cause discord and division among the brethren. It's all about self, and God says of this type of behavior, "I hate it" (see Proverbs 6:16, 19).

Lovers of Money

After their love of self, some false teachers are "lovers of money" (2 Timothy 3:2). First Timothy 6:5 tells us that many of these people see ministry as a means of financial gain. According to the New Testament, Christian ministers have a right to be financially supported, but false teachers engage in religious work to line their pockets by fleecing the flock. They will pray for you with one hand on your shoulder and the other in your wallet.

There are television, radio, and online ministries that pressure their followers by saying, "Help us keep our doors open or keep us on the air. Send us your money so that this ministry can continue. Act now!" Or, "Send in your seed money. Send in your seed of faith and God will bless you." That is heresy, my friend. Nowhere in the Bible does God say, "I need or want your money." Yet that is what these types of pleas suggest. It makes me want to shout back, "How about you act on your faith without taking money from anybody less fortunate, much less grandma and grandpa's pension check? Why don't you act on faith by practicing what you preach?" Many of these same teachers have become multimillionaires by ripping off the church. They are not afraid to parade their expensive suits, jewelry, watches, and lifestyles—they'll even brag about their prosperity!

I am not saying that God's ministers have got to live like paupers to be legitimate. Nor am I saying it is wrong for a church to ask congregants to worship through regular support of the church and its ministries. I am only pointing out those who use pressure tactics for giving, and asking you to do your homework and compare a teacher's statements to what you find in the Word of God.

Lovers of Pleasure Rather Than God

There are two loves in direct opposition to one another in the phrase "lovers of pleasure rather than lovers of God" (2 Timothy 3:4). One love entails accommodation and compromise, and the other, sanctification and holiness. Lover of pleasure describes a person who has chosen a life of ease and gratification rather than a wholehearted love of God. They have been deceived, like Balaam, into thinking they can embrace the world and somehow still serve God. I bring up Balaam because 2 Peter 2:15 links false prophets in the New Testament to this Old Testament prophet: "They have forsaken the right way and gone astray, following the way of Balaam the son of Beor, who loved the wages of unrighteousness."

Reading 2 Peter 2:15 in English sounds serious, but if you read it in the language of the New Testament—Koine Greek—that Peter spoke, the intensity of the words will send fear up your spine. This is a grave warning that no minister is beyond ending up like Balaam.

I encourage you to read the entire account of Balaam to help understand the gravity of Balaam's sin. But in short, the king of Moab, Balak, offered a bribe to Balaam to get him to curse God's people. The prophet knew he couldn't curse what God had not cursed (Numbers 23:8), so instead, he found a way to compromise and circumvent God's command, giving both he and Balak what each wanted. Balaam *taught* Balak to "put a stumbling block before the children of Israel, to eat things sacrificed to idols, and to commit sexual immorality" (Revelation 2:14; see Numbers 22:5–24:25).

Compromise has become a cancer within today's church and has led to the wasting away of what should be a healthy body of Christ. Who do you respect spiritually? Who has the Lord used to influence your life? Pray for them! Earnestly intercede for your pastor and your church. Pray they would remain strong and steadfast and not succumb to the 24/7 onslaught of satanic attacks against them.

Now would be a good time to stop and think about the pastors, churches, and ministries you support. If you feel uncomfortable doing so, it could be that you've realized that the people I've just described are among the ones you've been giving your God-given resources to. You liked their personality and program. You bought their bestselling book. But now, you need to decide whether to follow biblical truth or emotion. With so much deception happening in the name of Christ, we must exercise wisdom regarding who we support. I believe asking the following questions can be helpful:

- What are these people like when they're not in the pulpit or on stage? Are their lifestyles and attitudes in line with what they teach? Can you verify it?
- Do you know how they get around when they travel? Are they like everyone else, or do they seek special treatment?
- Do you know where the ministry's dollars go, and what percentage actually goes toward ministry?

YOU WILL KNOW THEM BY THEIR DESTRUCTIVE HERESIES

In places where the truth of God's Word is consistently taught, Scripture alerts us that eventually, false prophets and teachers will be there too. "There were also false prophets among the people, even as there will be false teachers among you, who will secretly bring in destructive heresies, even denying the Lord who bought them, and bring on themselves swift destruction" (2 Peter 2:1).

False teachers slip into congregations unnoticed. They are friendly, nice, often charismatic, and eager to get involved in positions of leadership—they're looking for those who don't know the Bible very well. Then, when the time is right, they go to work. Unless they are blatantly giving out false doctrine, the majority of what they teach is Bible truth, until they start slowly slipping in lies. They will suggest options or choices that are appealing yet have no biblical basis.

Choices are nice when ordering ice cream or pizza, but the Bible is clear that we don't get to order up our own flavor of doctrine. Take, for instance, the doctrine of salvation. When the Bible says there is only one way to heaven (John 14:6), it means there is only one way. But along comes the false teacher who pats your shoulder and says, "The Holy Spirit has given me a unique insight. I will show you how all roads lead to God if you are sincere." Technically, that person is right. All roads do lead to God in judgment, but only one leads to heaven.

Peter warned us that destructive heresies are brought in secretly. The Greek word used for "bring" implies that a messenger, minister, or pastor brings the information. Sincere people will knock on your door and present you with revelations they say were given to their prophets by God. I want to make it very clear that when it comes to the Christian faith, there are not going to be any new revelations. God has given us the Bible, and He is done speaking to us. How can we know for sure? God's Word says so.

> At various times and in various ways [God] spoke in time past to the fathers by the prophets, [but] has in these last days spoken to us by His Son (Hebrews 1:1-2).

And in Revelation 22:18-19, we read,

> I testify to everyone who hears the words of the prophecy of this book: If anyone adds to these things, God will add to him the plagues that are written in this book; and if anyone takes away from the words of the book of this prophecy, God shall take away his part from the Book of Life, from the holy city, and from the things which are written in this book.

God is adamant—the Bible is His final word. He is done talking.

Regarding the Deity of Jesus Christ

False teachers are predictable. They are always guilty of this one act: undermining the deity of Jesus Christ. The deity of Christ offends religious people and atheists alike. Those who adhere to New Age beliefs will agree that Jesus is God, but in the same breath, say, "So what? He is just another incarnation of deity. In fact, we're all gods." How convenient is that? If you're a god, you become the sole authority for running your life. You could even argue that because you are a god, you are exempt from answering to anyone regarding your actions. You have complete freedom to do as you please.

When God said, "Let Us make man in Our image, according to Our likeness" (Genesis 1:26), He created humans to be the expressed manifestation of His tangible nature. What this does not mean is that when God created humanity, He created a second tier or second level of deity. Adam and Eve were created perfectly, but they were in no way God—and neither are we.

As far as religious people go, Jehovah's Witnesses are a prime example of a group that falsely identifies themselves as Christian while undermining the deity of Christ. They believe that Jesus is a created being who is Michael the archangel in the Old Testament. In order to come to this conclusion, you must twist, turn, misinterpret, and reinterpret Scripture (see 2 Peter 3:16), which is exactly what they have done with their New World Translation of the Bible.

In the previous chapter, we saw how the Bible validates that Jesus is God, and though I don't want to belabor the point here, I want to give you a few more verses to have ready the next time that visitors from this, or any other, cult knock at your door. Remember, these are not man's opinions; these are what God's Word says.

> We know that the Son of God has come and has given us an understanding, that we may know Him who is true; and we are in Him who is true, in His Son Jesus Christ. This is the true God and eternal life (1 John 5:20).

> Without controversy great is the mystery of godliness:
> God was manifested in the flesh,

justified in the Spirit,
seen by angels,
preached among the Gentiles,
believed on in the world,
received up in glory (1 Timothy 3:16).

Looking for the blessed hope and glorious appearing of our great God and Savior Jesus Christ, who gave Himself for us, that He might redeem us from every lawless deed and purify for Himself His own special people, zealous for good works (Titus 2:13-14).

I also want to stress the serious consequences of the heresy that Jesus is not God. If that were true, then His sacrifice on the cross is not sufficient for your salvation, because only God could pay the penalty for sin. And if Christ's sacrifice is not sufficient, then that means you must earn your way to heaven—which nullifies the grace of God. Those who dismantle the deity of Jesus Christ also end up tearing down the grace of God.

Regarding the Grace of God

Grace is a tremendous word, so why do false teachers and prophets hate it so much? Because grace is available to everyone, not just a select few. The grace of God sets you free, gives you liberty, and provides spiritual power. Cults hate that, and false prophets won't stand for it.

Author Hal Lindsey has been widely quoted as the originator of a memorable acronym that I pray puts grace into perspective for you: G.R.A.C.E. = God's Riches At Christ's Expense.

Grace is God's unearned and unmerited favor. God loves you so much that every day, He supplies you with the breath that fills your lungs, the food on your table, and the clothes on your back. He cares about you! You may say, "But I worked for those things." The reality is this: God's favor provides you with the strength and ability to get up every morning and do what your day requires. He is the one who meets your needs.

Scripture tells us that the ultimate expression of God's grace is when He stepped into human skin and said, "I will pay all your sin-debt. My blood will wash you white as snow so you can enter heaven. You don't have to work for any of this. All of it will be paid for by Me." But the cults say, "No, that's not exactly true." They will agree that you are saved through faith, which you recognize from Ephesians 2:8-9. So, all is well, right?

> Scripture tells us that the ultimate expression of God's grace is when He stepped into human skin and said, "I will pay all your sin-debt."

Wrong! They go on to add, "You still need to do all you can." That, my friend, is the kind of doctrine taught by many other religious groups, including the Mormons. Paul warned believers about this perversion of the gospel in Galatians 1:6-8 and marveled at the way that some people turn away from grace. *The Expositor's Bible Commentary* explains it this way.

> The vehemence with which Paul denounces those who teach another gospel (literally, he says, "Let them be damned") has bothered some commentators, as well as other readers of the letter. But this shows *how little the gospel of God's grace is understood and appreciated* and how little many Christians are concerned for the advance of biblical truth.[1]

I want to paint a mental picture concerning grace that I hope you never lose. Imagine Jesus hanging on the cross and someone walking up and chopping off His leg. Then someone else removes a pectoral muscle, and another takes a carpenter's planer to His skin.

I know this leaves you with a bloody and brutal image, but that's how severely false doctrine dismantles the sacrificial atonement that Jesus Christ made on Calvary's cross. In my mind, that is exactly what happens every time someone says, "I can work my way into heaven." If that's you, and you believe that you've gotten your act together, you are not anywhere near the kingdom of God. Or if salvation in Jesus involves any kind of labor, chances are you've listened to the voice of a false prophet. Jesus said, "My yoke is easy and My burden is light" (Matthew 11:30).

Believer, every bit of the life that you enjoy in Christ is by grace alone. Grace plus works isn't an option. It is heresy, and God hates it.

A WARNING TO ALL

False teachers have only one goal: to steal or sterilize sheep. Jesus likened those who lead others astray to "thieves and robbers" (John 10:7-8). Sheep rustlers have been roaming the countryside as long as there have been sheep. In Jesus' day, when a thief crested a hill and found sheep grazing, he immediately knew what to do. This was just the opportunity he had been waiting for—and he was ready. With him was a goat trained to mingle among the unsuspecting sheep until it heard a certain whistle tone. At the sound, the goat would run around in such a way as to startle the sheep so that they would follow it back over the hill and through the small door of a prepared pen. The door would then be sealed, and the thief now had another man's flock in his possession.

Put that illustration into a church setting of today, and the result is startling, isn't it? Now you can see why maintaining sound doctrine is absolutely vital to the health and well-being of the body of Christ.

Jesus said, "The thief does not come except to steal, and to kill, and to destroy. I have come that they may have life, and that they may have it more abundantly" (John 10:10). False teachers want to rob you of your liberty and freedom in Christ and replace it with a counterfeit gospel and false doctrines that will lead into bondage. Don't let that become your fate.

We've looked at the deceptiveness of false teachers, but there are also teachers in wonderful positions with wonderful churches, and everything about them is wonderful by all appearances. Yet you can tell by either their pride, arrogance, or the content of their teaching that they have departed from a personal day-by-day walk with Jesus. They have neglected the systematic study of the Bible and consequently are susceptible to the deception of the false doctrines currently in vogue. Without a change of course, their faith will be shipwrecked, which is tragic. Equally tragic is that they will take many in their congregations down with them.

Perhaps you are one of those pastor-teachers or in one of those congregations. I want to share a story I heard years ago that underscores the importance of heeding the warning signals of God's Word.

On a foggy evening, a great battleship was steaming full speed ahead when those on the bridge saw a flash in the distance. Aboard was an admiral, who requested a crew member to flash a signal back to establish communication, which he did. The light flashed again. At that, the admiral said, "Communicate to that flash over there and tell them that we are the United States Navy."

A series of flashes was returned. "Stop advancing. Reverse your engines."

"Well, sir," the crewman said to the admiral, "he's saying stop advancing. Reverse our engines."

By now the admiral was indignant. "You tell that person on the other end that we are the United States Navy, and this is the greatest battleship of all time."

The reply came back, "Do not advance. Reverse engines. Back up."

"Admiral, sir, he's saying the same thing again."

"You tell him that I am the great Rear Admiral So and So, and we are the United States Navy. Nobody tells us to turn around. We're going full speed ahead. We are the authority in these open seas. We're the most powerful ship that has ever been built."

The crewmember obediently transmitted the admiral's message. There was a moment's pause before the light flashed again in response.

"I am Seaman First Class Jones, and this is a lighthouse!"

Seaman First Class Jones had no authority over Rear Admiral So and So, and if the admiral had wanted to, he could have taken that great ship and rammed it into the lighthouse. But the lighthouse was perched on an unmovable and sure foundation, be it a rock, an island, or the coast. Likewise, you are in one of two places today.

Either you are settled firmly on the rock of your salvation, Jesus Christ. You are trusting in the blood of Jesus and the grace of God to secure the gift of eternal life, which you received upon accepting Christ as your Savior. To you, I say continue growing "in the grace and knowledge of our Lord and Savior Jesus Christ" (2 Peter 3:18) until the day He comes to take you home.

Or you are sailing through life thinking you're okay, yet spiritually you are on a dangerous course, like that battleship. But God's truth is like that lighthouse, and you'll run into it someday. If that is you, I urge you, it is time to change course.

CHAPTER 3

DAZED BY DECEPTIVE SPIRITS

B ack in the late 1930s when television was still young, Americans fell in love with game shows. One of the longest-running shows, *To Tell the Truth*, was a big hit with viewers. In the show, three contestants—all claiming to be the same person with an unusual occupation or experience—were pitted against a panel of four celebrities. Two of the contestants lied their hearts out to evade detection as imposters, while the actual person simply told the truth. The panel's job was to ask the right questions and figure out which contestant was the real deal. As Christ-followers, isn't this the dilemma facing us today? Discovering who is telling the truth?

The question of how we know who is telling the truth leads us directly to 1 John 4:1-6. This portion of Scripture is fantastic for us as believers and, by the nature of its content, applies to our age. We will return to these six verses throughout the rest of this book, so let's get started.

> Beloved, do not believe every spirit, but test the spirits, whether they are of God; because many false prophets have gone out into the world. By this you know the Spirit of God:

> Every spirit that confesses that Jesus Christ has come in the flesh is of God, and every spirit that does not confess that Jesus Christ has come in the flesh is not of God. And this is the spirit of the Antichrist, which you have heard was coming, and is now already in the world.
>
> You are of God, little children, and have overcome them, because He who is in you is greater than he who is in the world. They are of the world. Therefore they speak as of the world, and the world hears them. We are of God. He who knows God hears us; he who is not of God does not hear us. By this we know the spirit of truth and the spirit of error.

Here in 1 John, an announcement is made that a division exists—it is spiritual, and it is going to manifest itself physically in a gathering of believers. Certainly, most who read the original letter had insight into the division John was referring to, but there were probably some who weren't quite sure what he was talking about. Have you noticed in your life that there are times when the Bible's teachings have challenged you to think and to ask questions? God loves it when we come to Him with our questions because He has answers for us (Isaiah 1:18).

I believe it is critical that we seek truth from the Word of God for this reason: the command to "test the spirits" requires it of us. Testing is an ongoing action of judging things against Scripture, and it presupposes a need within the body of Christ.

The church is a divine institution created by God and paid for by Christ's blood, yet internally, we are tempted to go astray. Sad to say, it's the human factor. When this surfaces within the church, there are inclinations to water down God's Word, not exercise church discipline, be lazy about doctrine, and ultimately, not be concerned about those things and more. Yet some believers prefer to turn a blind eye and a deaf ear to what is going on. To those people, I say, "Be careful." You are liable to end up like an ostrich I saw on a nature program.

The camera crew captured footage of that big bird running as fast as he could from a lion—until he saw a hole in the ground and stuck his head in. My first thought was, *Why?* Followed by, *What was he thinking?* Was it a case of denial? Was he saying, "If I don't see the lion, he can't see me"? Whatever it was, the ploy didn't work. The next thing I saw was a poof of dust and a plume of feathers in the air. What is the lesson here? Pretending something bad doesn't exist doesn't mean it can't hurt you.

ASK LOTS OF QUESTIONS

The late atheist Madalyn Murray O'Hair was labeled "the most hated woman in America."[1] Yet if she were alive today and she walked up to you and said, "I sued the government and forced school districts to remove prayer from your children's classrooms," would you feel threatened? How about if you were approached by a full-blown satanist wearing strange garb? I doubt you would feel intimidated by either of them because it is easy to see that their messages and beliefs are blatantly anti-Christian. In-your-face deception is easy to spot, but you might be shocked as to the degree that deception has permeated Christianity.

Wherever you find a work of God and the Holy Spirit having free reign to do as they will, you will find Satan, your enemy, at work. Let me remind you: Jesus had a little church of 12, and one of them had a diabolical plan.

The Bible says to scrutinize and exercise caution toward those who operate under the cloak of religion, specifically those identifying as pastors and ministry leaders. You should be able to question Christian leadership. Whenever you can't, you need to seriously evaluate whether it's best to get out of that church and steer clear of that ministry. I understand that ministry leaders must exercise wisdom in responding to questions because information can be twisted and distorted. But something is wrong when a church is secretive and cannot bear testing.

From this point forward in your Christian walk, I encourage you to think critically and ask many questions of the Bible itself, and of fellow believers. You can begin by asking:

Who should I be scrutinizing? In what settings will I see them?

What kinds of spirits does the Bible warn us about? What drives them?

What does it mean to test the spirits?

What should I do with my new knowledge?

Those are only a few of the questions you might want to ask. I am sure you can come up with more, so go for it!

DON'T BELIEVE EVERY SPIRIT
Erroneous Spirits

I hate to say it, but people form their doctrine from all sorts of places. Every year, usually around Easter, magazines run religious articles that would be laughable if they weren't so damaging. Some time ago, the cover story of *US News & World Report* was on hell.[2] The magazine's cover featured Satan dressed in a Hawaiian shirt and shorts, holding a tall drink topped by a cocktail umbrella. Hell's flames could be seen in the background while bikini-clad girls fanned an unconcerned man. According to the research cited in the article, hell was not as bad as previously thought.

On May 8, 2020, *Time* magazine ran an article entitled "What Jesus Really Said About Heaven and Hell" by a liberal professor of New Testament religious studies. In the article, the author put his own spin on Jesus' teaching on hell by merging it with that of Socrates's. His conclusion? We now know that hell isn't what we've been taught. How convenient for Satan, and deceptive for those bound up in their sin.

Whether readers realized it or not, the moment they finished reading either of those articles, they were confronted with a test. Do I buy into the belief that hell isn't worth all the fuss, or believe what the Bible says? Jesus said hell is a real place of eternal torment where there is "weeping and gnashing of teeth" and "the maggots never die and the fire never goes out" (Luke 13:28; Mark 9:48 NLT). He died so that you don't have to go there.

You need to ask yourself: Who stands to gain if I toss out the inerrant Word of God, live as I please, and inherit the horrors of hell? And why did Jesus go to the cross if hell is an acceptable alternative to heaven?

Judge for yourself which is the spirit of truth, and which is the spirit of error.

Lying Spirits

Jesus warned believers that as the end of the age draws near, "Take heed that no one deceives you. For many will come in My name, saying, 'I am the Christ,' and will deceive many" (Matthew 24:5). The Greek word translated "name" means "authority." There have been and still are men who proclaim themselves to be the Messiah and deceive many. But there are many more claiming to have the authority to speak as Jesus' representative. The apostle Paul called them "false apostles, deceitful workers, transforming themselves into apostles of Christ" (2 Corinthians 11:13). Wow! The same Paul who wrote that harsh condemnation also penned the poetic verses on love that we read in 1 Corinthians 13. If you think love is complete acceptance of everything and everyone, you will label Paul a hypocrite. But true love is telling it like it is so that people don't follow a path to destruction.

Several years ago, I had the honor of being part of a group of advisers to the Department of Homeland Security regarding the threat of radical Islam and how Islamists view the West—specifically, the United States. We were focused on the constant threat that the country faces regarding the quiet and sometimes almost invisible infiltration of extremists seeking to destroy the United States from the inside. Within that group, the prevailing standard was that if anything was seen, it must be said. As we worked together, I couldn't help but notice that the standard being utilized lined up perfectly with Paul's and others' warnings. In other words, if you see something, say something.

Paul called spiritual imposters "false," or as the original text says in Greek, *pseudo*. In English, we understand the word *pseudo* to mean "not genuine." Spiritually speaking, it means to be a pretender and, interestingly, an off-course instructor. Deceitful workers know they are off course and willfully lead their students even further off course than themselves, making them "twice as much a son of hell" (Matthew 23:15).

Paul wasn't content to stop at exposing the false teachers whom Jesus called "ravenous wolves in sheep's clothing" (see Matthew 7:15). He pulled back their masks and looked under their wool, showing us the spirit behind the pretenders—he revealed their boss. Paul said it's no wonder that false teachers can do what they do: "For Satan himself transforms himself into an angel of light. Therefore it is no great thing if his ministers also transform themselves into ministers of righteousness" (2 Corinthians 11:14-15). It's true—Satan can change his outward appearance, but it is impossible for him to change what and who he really is, and the same is true of his workers. It's like me deciding to revamp my front yard by digging out the beautiful redwoods and replacing them with desert cacti. I've achieved a whole new look, but the fact remains it's still my yard.

Demonic Spirits

There are literal spirits—demonic entities—driving the incredible amount of false doctrine and other forms of deception in the world today. You and I cannot see them, nor do we want to, but they are real. In Job 1:7, we read, "The LORD said to Satan, 'From where do you come?' So Satan answered the LORD and said, 'From going to and fro on the earth, and from walking back and forth on it.'" Concrete and metal cannot restrict Satan's movements. He can pass through buildings and cars. He roams the earth, and he is working right now to derail your life and mine. Satan wants to keep us from living as lights and witnesses to the world.

You could be reading this, thinking, *Okay, I get what you're saying. But so what? I'm fine.* Don't be deceived! Demonic attacks don't always come as a full-on assault. They often sneak up when we least expect them. Maybe you can relate to this scenario. You are in church, all dressed up, feeling fine, and praising the Lord. You could even be singing "How Great Thou Art," but you're a bit preoccupied and your mind starts to wander. The next thing you know, your thoughts jump someplace they shouldn't go. Whoa! What just happened? Demonically driven thoughts and emotions.

Like a spider, Satan was subtly spinning a web long before this moment—this is how he operates. Part of the devil's craftiness is lulling you into believing you are doing just fine while he is quietly at work. He does his best to weave lies into and around your heart, mind, spirit, and soul, to the point where he has you bound and captive.

If the thought of demonically driven deception scares you, this is what you need to remember: "He who is in you is greater than he who is in the world" (1 John 4:4). And "God has not given us a spirit of fear, but of power and of love and of a sound mind" (2 Timothy 1:7).

TEST ALL THINGS

By now, you might be wondering, *How can I know whether my thoughts and beliefs, or the ideas of others, are from God or not?* Great question. The answer comes as you put those thoughts or ideas to the test.

Most people have heard about the California Gold Rush. Miners from all over the world arrived in search of riches, but they could never be sure what they had found was real until the assayer put their bag of rocks to the test. Far too many discovered that not everything that glittered was gold. Those poor souls' gold turned out to be pyrite—fool's gold—which looks precious but is worthless.

Likewise, the only way to know whether what you believe is as fine gold or worthy of the trash heap is to act as an assayer and put it to the test. John's admonishment in 1 John 4:1 to "test the spirits" is the same as Paul's word to the Thessalonian believers to "test all things" (1 Thessalonians 5:21). What does "all" mean? *All!*

Test What You Hear

No matter what language you speak, a specific word can have a variety of meanings. Take, for instance, the word *spam*. Spam is a canned meat product, yet someone with a sense of humor adapted the term as slang for junk email in your inbox. But unlike legitimately different usages of words, we see a determined effort today by some people to manipulate and redefine words and concepts so they can create narratives to suit their purposes. We saw this with the antics of a former president and how easily he altered the definition of *sex*. Whenever a media interviewer tried to pin him down on what he meant, he gave a definition that wasn't the true meaning of the word. People rolled their eyes and news agencies mocked him because he stuck with his false definition. But the more this usage was repeated, the more his narrative became culturally accepted.

Similar redefinition leads to errors in science. For instance, when eminent paleontologist and biologist Steven Gould talked about the definition of *science*, he said, "Science has its subject—the material world—and religion its—moral discourse—and each leaves the other plenty of elbow room."[3] If you dig deeper into Gould's personal beliefs, you can see how they informed his new definition, making it compatible with the fallacy of evolution. For centuries, scientists have believed that self-evident, empirical truths form the foundation of pure science, which makes the *theory* of evolution impossible. Stephen Gould's attempts to redefine science conveniently fit his personal narrative but cannot withstand scrutiny.

Redefining words isn't limited to the secular world; religious cults have been doing it for years. They have lifted terms like *born again*, *Spirit-filled*, and *doctrine* right out of biblical Christianity and are using a different dictionary to define them. I wish that I could say falsehoods are limited to cults, but they aren't. Mainstream Christianity is witnessing a lot of division, and I don't mean along denominational lines, although that is certainly true as well. The chasm is widening between truth and error in many areas.

Exercising critical listening and thinking skills is essential when we hear statements like, "I'm going to tonight's crusade because the speaker is so charismatic." *Charismatic* is a great word. I hope that you and I are considered charismatic because it means the ability to inspire people.

There is nothing wrong with being charismatic, but the deception comes in when you step inside a "charismatic" service, hear someone speak in a supposedly unknown tongue, and a spoken message is given as the interpretation. Wrong! Right then and there, what took place is immediately outside of the Word and will of God. How do we know? First Corinthians 14:2 says that the person exercising the gift of speaking in tongues is not speaking to men but to God. So, it naturally follows that the interpretation would not be a message to the congregation but rather a prayer, praise, or thanksgiving to God.

Are you willing to walk out of such a service? I pray so. But, unfortunately, the daze of deceptive spirits allows people to go to churches, week in and week out, without ever questioning whether what they are participating in is right according to Scripture.

Test What You See

The saying "Seeing is believing" sounds like it could have come from a modern-day ad campaign, but the idea originated with the ancient Greeks. The Greeks thought seeing and knowing were one and the same. Today, we would say, "Hey, I saw it with my own eyes, so it's got to be true." Not always.

When Paul warned about false teachers, he likened them to Pharaoh's magicians, Jannes and Jambres (2 Timothy 3:8). Why? When Moses threw his staff on the ground and it became a snake, who caused the staff to turn into a snake? God did. When Jannes and Jambres imitated Moses and their sticks turned into snakes, who did it? Satan. Seeing shouldn't always result in believing.

In the last days, people will follow signs and lying wonders according to the working of Satan. Again, please understand this: a very real, exceedingly powerful, and incredibly beautiful evil is approaching that is unlike anything this world has ever seen. And keep in mind that its motive is always deceit. So, imagine if you were to see a child without a hand and some guy prays in a name other than Jesus', and a hand starts growing. Would you start following that person because you saw something allegedly supernatural happen, or would you test the situation with biblical doctrine?

Let me bring this closer to home. You have cancer, with no hope of recovery. There is a man down the street who is not preaching a biblical Jesus, but he is hosting a healing service. It has been reported that people have been healed, including some who have your type of cancer. Would you go? Would the possibility of having your cancer removed cause you to flush Bible doctrine down the drain? That is the test.

In every one of the above instances—from what you hear to what you see—your job is to investigate and make sure that you're speaking the same spiritual language. You need a discerning spirit that listens carefully, judges doctrinally, and tests everything against God's Word. Remember when Satan twisted scripture in an attempt to get Jesus to make bread from a stone (Luke 4:3)? Understanding good theology and sound doctrine isn't only for pastors and church leaders. They are *your* tools for testing the spirits.

STAY CENTERED

You and I are watching people whom we thought were committed Christians fall to our left and right, both doctrinally and spiritually. So how do we stay safe and sound, in the center, with the Lord? It comes down to this: You and I must stand fast in truth, which is not of human origin, but comes from God alone. The way that we remain in His truth is the same for every believer. There isn't one way for the spiritually mature and another for babes in Christ. All of us come empty-handed before God's throne in need of help.

I want to share with you some ways you can be sure to stay in God's truth, with the hope that these guidelines will help you understand how to effectively test the spirits.

Stay Centered by Judging Rightly

In today's culture, it is imperative that we as Christians operate at a high standard. By that I mean we must be on guard and alert because everything around us has a spiritual significance behind it. There is nothing in our lives that is without meaning. I firmly believe that God wastes not one moment—not one event, action, or situation—and neither does Satan. That alone is good reason for you and me to judge rightly, as Jesus commanded in John 7:24: "Do not judge according to appearance, but judge with righteous judgment."

The Bible says we are to judge, but never by human standards. We are to resist any form of self-righteousness. We are to avoid being harsh, critical, fault-finding, and legalistic. We have no authority nor any right to condemn anyone, but when we are guided by the Holy Spirit, we will draw discerning conclusions. It is the Spirit who must lead and guide us in that endeavor. Jesus promised, "I will pray the Father, and He will give you another Helper, that He may abide with you forever—the Spirit of truth, whom the world cannot receive, because it neither sees Him nor knows Him; but you know Him, for He dwells with you and will be in you" (John 14:16-17).

> When we take in the Word of God, clear and clean as presented by Him, it serves as a glistening, brilliant light that enables us to conduct our lives according to His will with boldness.

So, believer, as you go about your daily business, will you make it your habit to probe the issues that are before you, and listen with an attentive ear to what others are saying? Will you ask the Spirit to give you the discernment to understand what is taking place around you so that you can judge what is beneficial and what to avoid? Will you compare and contrast—or judge—all things according to the Word of God?

Stay Centered by Searching Diligently

Deceiving spirits are not going to show up and say, "Hi. We're here to deceive you." You, like all believers, must make a determined search of the Scriptures to figure out whether a teacher is true or false. I want you to include me and my teaching in that search as well. I love hearing from someone who says, "Jack, I went home after church and studied what you taught." That is exactly what Paul commended the believers for in Acts 17:11, and it warms this pastor's heart.

Ultimately, God's truth is the only truth that will save us, preserve us, and keep us from stumbling. When we take in the Word of God, clear and clean as presented by Him, it serves as a glistening, brilliant light that enables us to conduct our lives according to His will with boldness. His Word helps to dispel the daze generated by deception.

> The more familiar you are with the whole counsel of God, the more quickly truth becomes visible.

I remember when I was a young Christian and I bought my first Bible. I was so thrilled to start reading God's Word! But impatient me, I wanted to know how everything turned out. So I started with the last book, Revelation. As I studied Revelation, I quickly became aware that I was touring the Old Testament. That's right: The 404 verses of Revelation either point to or are based on about 280 verses from the Old Testament. That level of immersion in Scripture proved extremely important in the early days of my Christian life, as it does now. Please never regard any part of God's Word as unimportant!

In Psalm 138:2, we read that God magnifies His Word above His name. I love this truth! It elevates the things of God and reminds me that His Word is to be number one in my life. I use the Bible to judge everything, including my thought life, imagination, conversations, and conduct, both privately and publicly. When God's Word rules and reigns, my emotions and feelings are placed on the back burner. It takes all of what is me and makes it a lower priority (Matthew 6:33; John 3:30).

Likewise, searching the Scriptures is vital to your spiritual success. Get yourself a good concordance and Bible dictionary and learn how to use them. Coupled with your Bible, they will help you lay down line upon line of sound doctrine. The more familiar you are with the whole counsel of God, the more quickly truth becomes visible. Scripture shows us the heart and mind—the very will—of God. It is the guide for what to look for, how to look, and what to do when you see it. When armed this way, you are less likely to stumble.

Stay Centered by Fasting and Praying

There are times in our Christian experience when we just don't seem to be getting answers to our questions. We can't see clearly, and everything feels odd, even crushing to our soul. We read the Bible, but it seems silent; we cry out to God, and it's as though He is not listening. What's going on? In situations like this, we need to call up special reinforcements—we must fast and pray. In a sense, this means going into special operations mode so we can resist the forces of darkness.

Fasting deprives us of routines we gravitate toward because they are appealing and comforting. I'm not talking about going without lunch; that could easily be called a diet. Fasting isn't necessarily about depriving ourselves of food, although not eating can be a part of it. But it could involve how we spend our breaks at work or leisure time at home.

The fast that I am talking about is a time of devotion and dedication that seeks God's direction. It results in the Holy Spirit supernaturally taking hold of your life as you pray and read the Scriptures, giving you a profound clarity about what to do. You become doubly focused—laser-like—as you pray. It's quite remarkable. By denying the physical body, your spirit becomes more attentive to the Holy Spirit, who prepares you to receive answers to your questions. And as you pray, He shows you what to do next.

The intent of prayer is not to try to change the mind of God. By no means. Rather, prayer aligns us with God's plan and purpose. To understand this better, read the account of Jesus' prayer in the garden of Gethsemane and how He aligned His will with the Father's. From that moment on, notice the power and clarity with which He moved forward. Notice the unwavering devotion that Jesus showed as He went to His crucifixion. Scripture tells us that the great victory of our salvation was purchased at the cross. But it was determined in the garden of Gethsemane. There, Jesus' will surrendered to the glorious redemptive plan of God.

Stay Centered by Praying Always

I like to live with the mentality that the Lord and I have a perpetual, never-ending conversation going between just the two of us. To me, that's what the Bible means when it says to pray always. I can't describe the thrill that comes from keeping God constantly in my thoughts and knowing that I can approach Him anytime and bring my concerns and observations to Him. Sometimes I wonder if God might be thinking, *Jack, can you be quiet? Just for a moment?* That's how ongoing our conversation is.

I hate to admit it, but that wasn't always my perspective. There was a time when I thought the only time God could hear me was when I was in a very, very dedicated state of prayer. For the first three years of my Christian life, I prayed daily from 4:00 a.m. to 7:00 a.m., believing God wanted that from me. And anytime I couldn't keep that commitment, for one reason or another, I was so discouraged, disappointed, and even disgusted with myself.

Well, my dear friend, I want you to know that God, in His goodness, broke down my dependence on self-action and self-effort. The

Lord showed me, "Jack, I am with you always, even to the end of the age." He taught me, as He did Joshua, "I am with you wherever you go, be strong and of good courage" (see Joshua 1:9). Now I have complete freedom to pray whenever and wherever, which is not to say that I don't designate times when I'm alone with the Lord. I meet with God regularly in the early morning hours when it is silent, still, and dark. Those are sweet times that I love, relish, protect, and defend.

I hope that you make an effort to set aside a time and place to talk with God regularly. But even more than that, I urge you to develop an attitude of prayer. Once prayer becomes your ongoing mindset, I guarantee you'll find victory, joy, and discernment.

In these days of deception, let God always be Lord in your life (see Proverbs 3:5-6), and He will speak to you. He will enable you to discern what is true or false, right or wrong, and what you should draw close to or resist.

> Now to Him who is able to keep you from stumbling, and to present you faultless before the presence of His glory with exceeding joy, to God our Savior, who alone is wise, be glory and majesty, dominion and power, both now and forever. Amen (Jude 24-25).

CHAPTER 4

DAZED BY DOCTRINES OF DEMONS

You may believe that all doctrine is good and limited to the church, but I urge you to think again. The subject of the doctrines of demons is like one of those enormous golf umbrellas—it can cover a broad area. Satan's ability to infuse our world with lies has turned what God says is detestable into what people say is acceptable. This is the only way to explain the twisted ideologies we are witnessing today. These aren't new and improved ways, only a regurgitation of the teachings of demons. If you understand that concept, you will be empowered. You will be able to identify whether ideas and beliefs are of God or come under the umbrella of the doctrines of demons.

WHOSE DOCTRINE IS IT?

The apostle Paul warned his young protégé, Timothy, that the last days would be times of great deception. We now know that some deceptions are obvious, while others are much more subtle and, therefore, more dangerous. Paul called them "doctrines of demons" (1 Timothy 4:1). The word "doctrine" comes from the Greek word *didaskalia*. It means information imparted by a teacher coupled with their authority to instruct.

The need to exercise care when it comes to doctrine is rooted in the fact that information is one of your most valuable possessions. That raises the question: What about faith, peace, love, or any other important attributes that Christians can possess? Certainly, those are near the top of the list. But those attributes become ours only after we've accepted God's authority as our teacher and applied information from His Word to our lives.

In my day, public schoolteachers often came across as strict or somewhat of a disciplinarian when they wanted to keep students on the straight and narrow. Their commitment wasn't always appreciated, but would they be a good teacher if it weren't for their dedication to seeing their students excel?

In certain circumstances, we might view God as that type of teacher, but it is important to remember that He is fully committed to our best. His instruction on the path we should take is straight, and yes, it is narrow (Matthew 7:14). Yet His path guarantees protection and promise. His ways offer pleasantness and peace (see Proverbs 3:17). But when and if we feel that isn't true, we'll make the mistake of taking the paths of another teacher, Satan himself.

When we accept the authority of the wrong teacher, we head down a path paved with deception and lies. No wonder we end up dazed, confused, and unable to determine which way to go. The devil's doctrines lure us into the proverbial weeds, leaving us to wonder, *Where am I?*

I also want to point out that not all teaching is verbal. Many of life's lessons are caught, not taught. Think about it. When you see a person engaged in an activity or living in a way that appeals to you, aren't you more inclined to follow their example? But before you do, you should ask yourself: What is their example teaching me, and where will it ultimately end?

From the garden of Eden until now, Satan's goal remains the same:

to disconnect and redirect humanity away from its Creator. Satan has achieved this with some success, but recently, he has leveraged some factors to his advantage.

DOCTRINE IN DIFFICULT DAYS

Paul, in his second letter to Timothy, said, "Know this, that in the last days perilous times will come" (2 Timothy 3:1). That is a powerful statement. The word "know" is a command, not a suggestion. Paul was saying, "Timothy, God commands you and all who come after you to know that perilous times will characterize the last days." If you read the verse in the original Greek language, you'll see that perilous times are those that slowly grind you down. Perilous times won't be limited to Christians, but will be a global phenomenon.

The word "perilous" brings out the idea of stress or being stressed on every front and from every angle. It means to push hard against another object. Perilous times will wear on you like a carpenter's plane shaving a piece of lumber one stroke at a time. In my mind's eye, I see a carpenter in his shop, and on his worktable is a small piece of wood that has his complete attention. For argument's sake, we'll call the wood your life and mine. The carpenter grabs the planer with both hands, and with every slow push, he shaves off a fresh curl of wood. Each curl is labeled. Some are sons, daughters, and parents; others are finances, health (both physical and mental), and circumstances. Each stroke represents an aspect of wear and tear upon your life.

Paul's personal experiences made him keenly aware of the danger of continual stress. He knew how easy it is to throw your hands up and say, "It's all too much. I just don't care anymore." Paul also understood how stress can make people more susceptible to the doctrines of demons, which is why he said, "Know this!" We need to take this admonishment and use it to our advantage. Knowing that the hard things in life are tools being used by our enemy will garrison our hearts against the lies that inevitably accompany them.

The World Is Shifting

Every person has a worldview—beliefs that form the foundation of how they see life and their understanding of right and wrong, good and bad, acceptable and unacceptable—in a word, morality. But when we fallible humans take our personal opinions and formulate our own truths, we move away from the rock-solid absolutes of God, who is infallible.

Here in Southern California, along the rugged Palos Verdes Peninsula is a section of coastline called Portuguese Bend. It is beautiful, and like other areas of California's coast, it looks far different than it did 100 years ago. The top layer of the headlands is slumping toward the Pacific Ocean. It is crumbling away. The terrain on which the roadway sits is so unpredictable that the Department of Transportation erected a warning sign for drivers: Use Extreme Caution—constant land movement next 0.8 miles.

Geologists tell us that Portuguese Bend is an area that has been active since ancient times, but their immediate concern is the current shift in the terrain. Multimillion-dollar homes, eateries, shops, and the Trump National Golf Club are all heading west into the Pacific Ocean. The ground is on the move, but stand in any of those spots, and you won't feel a thing. In fact, the distractions of waves, sunshine, and the occasional dolphin or whale spouting will lull you into a false sense of comfort and safety.

What is happening in Portuguese Bend mirrors what is happening in our world today. An imperceptible shift has been taking place under the foundations and pillars upon which we once stood. It is now apparent that the ground beneath us is giving way.

The Church Is Shifting

In recent years, George Barna's research polls have shown that a vast majority of Americans claim to believe in God. Yet when asked probing

questions about their doctrinal beliefs, the conclusions are dishearten-
ing, to say the least.

The institutional behemoths of religion have cut themselves loose from
the anchor of the great doctrines of the Bible. Few have noticed, and
even fewer have bothered to care. Record numbers of those who attend
these mainstream churches have no real understanding of the biblical
doctrines regarding the nature of God, Jesus Christ, or the Holy Spirit.
Even the doctrines of a literal heaven and hell are viewed as questionable.

In Western cultures, Christianity has fallen victim to those who are
supposed to be its custodians. Instead of pulpits filled with preachers,
pastors, and prophets, we now have traders and marketeers of religion
who promote anything and everything in the name of Christ.

The attacks on sound doctrine leave behind churches that are more
passionate about Black Lives Matter and feminism than the bedrock of
the Word of God. They care more about social justice than God's judgment and the gospel that saves mankind from it. Some churches are moving away from solid ground at such an alarming rate that there should
be warning signs posted over their doorways. Weak, ineffective churches
are of little value in the world in which God has placed them. They have
no ability to fight against the destructive doctrines that threaten those
whom they claim to care about.

There is good news, though: A small but dynamic change is taking
place. Compromise in various pulpits is forcing many to depart from
these mainstream denominations to find their source of spiritual strength
and discipleship in churches and small groups that are faithful to God's
Word. Christians are awakening to the fact that no matter how glorious
a ministry or church may appear on the outside, a sinister aspect, invisible to the naked eye, may be present on the inside. In a world dazed by
deception, vigilance is needed. We need to pay attention to the signs that
will expose the enemy's hidden agendas. The evidences of his plots and
plans are present—if we make the time to take a good look.

DOCTRINES FIT FOR A MODERN WORLD

Subversion

Satan is wily. He knows it isn't in his best interests to act in an outward, bombastic manner. There is no doubt that he can and sometimes does act this way, but when it comes to how he spreads his doctrines, usually he does it gradually and slowly. His methodology is subversion. If you could sum up what is happening in America and abroad, I think *subversion* is an excellent word to use.

According to the *Oxford Languages* website[1], subversion is the undermining of the power and authority of an established system or institution. We see this kind of activity happening all over the world. Good governance allows citizens to live and prosper in a way that strengthens a nation and makes it great—that is, until subversive practices take hold.

The kinds of subversive activities that undermine a country's foundation are spreading into all areas of society. This has led a growing number of people to ask, "How in the world did we get here?" Well, it wasn't overnight. It wasn't by the flip of a switch.

Progressivism in Education

Satan has covertly operated for decades in education under the guise of progressivism, or what some would like us to believe is a new reality. Progressivism's subversive doctrines have been entrenched on college and university campuses for so long that we hardly recognize them for what they are—a reformation of society that leaves God out of the picture. Sadly, these doctrines have now filtered down into the lower levels of public school systems. In the US, correct mathematical answers are considered racist, and bizarre pronoun usage has mangled the English language. On top of that, recent generations of students are woefully ignorant about American government and history.

Some may be surprised by the fact that a major aspect of America's greatness originated during the Revolutionary period. The colonists were steeped in education, beginning with the youngest ages. Literacy was at a higher standard and rate than that of Mother England herself.[2] What was the textbook many colonists used for reading? The Bible. The Puritans valued the ability to read and interpret Scripture. In fact, Massachusetts passed the Old Deluder Satan Act in 1647, which laid the foundation for the creation of public schools.

Of course, some argue that our "enlightened" culture has become so advanced that we have arrived. We don't need the Bible, nor do we need the Ten Commandments posted in our classrooms. I believe that if we have arrived at anything, it is a higher level of ignorance. Without moral guidance and spiritual truth, our children are destined to do the same as Israel of old, when "everyone did what was right in his own eyes" (Judges 17:6).

By God's design, parents are to be the primary source of influence in a child's life, yet today, many teachers and administrators are circumventing parental authority. When parents become privy to what is happening in schools, they are told to cede control of their children's lives because, after all, educators know best. Anytime a group or individual wants to relieve parents of the responsibility God has given to them, you know that a demonic doctrine is behind it.

Whether it's in government or on campuses, you can see the influence of progressive doctrines. From stoking imagined inequalities to magnifying real problems, society is now filled with volatile issues. Discord and misinformation are robbing us of civility and tolerance. But why should Satan stop there? He won't. And he hasn't.

Social Media

In the beginning, social media seemed primarily beneficial and perfectly harmless. People took to it for all the good it promised. What they didn't bargain for and certainly didn't see coming was the dark side—emotional addiction.

Social media has done more to usher in a crippling dependence upon the approval of others than anything else in human history to date. It consumes our thought life in a perpetual, nonstop thinking about self, which is now considered normal. This can be seen in how it has engulfed our children. Kids, especially teens, are conditioned to care about and respond to how absolute strangers view their media posts. This has become an effective tool for Satan because it causes a person to be highly vulnerable to the opinions and critiques of others. This, in turn, can result in significant damage to children's psychological and spiritual development. But kids weren't the first to be overtaken. Adults led the way.

Adults are not immune to the debilitating fear of others that social media's self-centered, self-absorbed thinking breeds. In its mildest form, it results in a narcissistic, domineering lifestyle, but it can easily go further. When people elevate themselves as the center of their universe, they eventually find it necessary to control others to maintain their spot as number one. This kind of environment breeds not only bullies but also despots and dictators. Now, compare this to the fear tactics of socialism, communism, or other forms of totalitarianism. Tyrants thrive on intimidation. If they can maintain a heightened state of fear, they can keep people in bondage. That is the purpose of the doctrines of demons as well.

Spirituality

After 30-plus years of public ministry, I have concluded there are primarily two secular viewpoints on life. One is that it is meaningless and lacking purpose. The other is that, by all accounts, life is an accident. Both are the hopeless worldviews of atheistic evolutionists. What atheists fail to recognize is that their unbelief severely limits their view—to the point of blindness. They cannot see the deep spiritual meaning and design of life, which makes them unable to see God. Thus, the unbelief of atheism is a doctrine of demons.

Unbelief is Satan's attempt to get people believing in anything other than the God of the Bible. When you read Scripture, especially the Old Testament, it is apparent that humanity has a propensity to worship something. Be honest: When you've questioned someone on their spiritual beliefs, have you ever met a person who truly believes in nothing? I can confidently say that those who claim to believe in nothing subscribe to an alternate theology. That theology may be the deification of self or the belief that science holds all the answers. Whatever that thing is, it has become the god of their belief system. It may take some probing to discover who or what a person's god is, but we need to let go of the idea that people who don't believe in God simply believe in nothing.

Sexuality

We live in a time when people desire to be spiritual while simultaneously avoiding the clear teachings of Scripture. This is perhaps most evident in the explosion of aberrant sexuality that the Bible warned would occur in the last days. We could point to many perversions, but I will choose just one—the idea that you can choose whether you are male or female based on your feelings or external suggestions and pressures. From the standpoint of biology alone, this is inconceivable. But the growing acceptance of this deviant sexual thinking renders Genesis chapter 1 no longer viable in the minds of many. In establishing male and female, God gave us the ability to procreate according to our biological gender. This miraculous, observable, repeatable, scientific, and theological fact is still true to this day and will always be true.

Sexuality is given by God not only to celebrate but to honor. On the other hand, Satan has perverted sexuality and redefined it in his plot to destroy what God called good. Why would this be so important to him? Because it undermines the very structure God has given for the design of man—and that includes Mr. and Mrs. Mankind.

Tragically, this is happening at an unprecedented rate on a global scale. It is yet another doctrine of demons.

Science

The idea that alternatives to biological humans might exist, in the form of aliens, has held humanity spellbound for millennia. Our current preoccupation with visitors from other worlds and unexplained phenomena fits perfectly with biblical warnings. From Erich von Daniken's book *Chariots of the Gods?* to the United States Air Force's latest reported sighting of a potential UFO, there is an underlying belief that we are not alone.

Jesus said that before His return, there would be signs in the heavens in conjunction with great deception among the nations and peoples of the world (see Matthew 24:24, 29-30). When people point to having witnessed something strange in the sky or claim to have seen a manifestation of an alternate life form, I am not quick to discount their statement. I believe that for many of them, what they are reporting is an event they experienced. This immediately reminds me of the necessity of testing the spirits because not all of them are of God.

I am not denying the thrill that comes from watching a 3-D sci-fi movie or reading a captivating book like *Fahrenheit 451* by Ray Bradbury. What I find interesting is that, by and large, those who give credence to these tales and accounts refuse to entertain any thought of God, who dwells outside of time and space. They are looking for a way out of having to face the eternal God, the Alpha and Omega, the Beginning and the End (Revelation 22:13).

Have you seen the pattern yet? In every area of life, Satan opens his Pandora's box of deviant beliefs and behaviors that undermine all that God has said is good, right, and normal.

DOCTRINE IS A MATTER OF LIFE AND DEATH

Why is it important to unmask the deceptive doctrines of demons? The short answer is because it is a matter of life and death.

I was once approached by a young girl—she was maybe 12 years old—after a Sunday message. She said, "You said something about the Watch Tower Society. I've been reading their magazine, and it makes a lot of sense to me." She stood there with such confidence, but my heart broke for her. She was being misled, and to help her recognize this, I said, "Imagine you are standing here with a compass in your hand that you plan on using to go to New York. But there is a problem. It is off by one degree. Sounds trivial, right? But that compass will never take you to New York. You will end up in Pennsylvania!" She might have thought, *Well, at least I'll be close.* When it comes to truth, however, being close isn't close enough.

The tragic ending to New Zealand Air Flight 901 demonstrates what happens when people rely on faulty information to take them to their desired destination.

> In 1979 a passenger jet carrying 257 people left New Zealand for a sightseeing flight to Antarctica and back. Unknown to the pilots, however, there was a minor 2-degree error in the flight coordinates. This placed the aircraft 28 miles to the east of where the pilots thought they were. As they approached Antarctica, the pilots descended to a lower altitude to give the passengers a better look at the landscape. Although both were experienced pilots, neither had made this particular flight before. They had no way of knowing that the incorrect coordinates had placed them directly in the path of Mount Erebus, an active volcano that rises from the frozen landscape to a height of more than 12,000 feet (3,700 m). Sadly, the plane crashed into the side of the volcano, killing everyone on board. It was a tragedy brought on by a minor error—a matter of only a few degrees.[3]

Satan is smart. He wants to get people to deviate just enough in their thinking to get them off course, and if there isn't a course correction, the result will be catastrophic.

Why God Cares

Doctrines that pervert the truth about God's nature, character, and intentions never exist in a vacuum—they naturally give birth to false worship. Both false doctrine and false worship are straight out of the doctrines of demons' playbook.

If we want to understand how God views those who practice and promote demonic doctrines, we can look to the Old Testament. Perhaps one of the most famous recorded events of God dealing with false prophets who worshipped pagan gods transpired between one prophet of God, Elijah, and 450 prophets of Baal atop Mount Carmel in Israel. There, the prophet of God stood alone, seemingly defenseless against the massive gathering of false prophets. Elijah laid down the ultimate challenge: "You call on the name of your gods, and I will call on the name of the LORD; and the God who answers by fire, He is God" (1 Kings 18:24).

The prophets of Baal built their altar and laid a sacrifice on top. All day long, they danced around and called out to their gods. But there was a deafening silence from above. So they began to cut themselves, as was their custom, until their blood gushed out. Still, nothing happened.

Then Elijah built a different altar—he rebuilt a broken-down altar of the Lord. He laid a sacrifice on top and doused everything three times with water until it overflowed from the altar's trenches. Satisfied, the great prophet called upon the one true God, whose response was an overwhelming manifestation of divine power. His presence came down with fire and "consumed the burnt sacrifice, and the wood and the stones and the dust, and it licked up the water that was in the trench" (1 Kings 18:38). This is the living God, the one who always has been and always will be—He is the Lord! "And Elijah said to them, 'Seize the prophets of Baal! Do not let one of them escape!' So they seized them; and Elijah brought them down to the Brook Kishon and executed them there" (verse 40).

Deuteronomy chapters 13 through 19 describe God's exacting

standards for prophets. God made it clear that if a prophet delivered a false message, his punishment would be death. Some might cringe and say that was too extreme, but I would argue that they view it that way because they do not fully appreciate what's at risk.

Why was God so harsh when He judged those who promoted demonic doctrines? Why not just leave them alone to perish in their deceived state? An indifferent opinion concerning false doctrine will see death as a radical or out-of-control remedy, even for God. But, again, the only reason people come to such a conclusion is that they do not view what is at stake the way that God does. False doctrine leads people astray, and when fully embraced, it condemns them to hell.

It was never God's intention for humans to occupy the corridors of hell. He created hell for Lucifer, his fallen angels, and the demonic spirits that work for them. Tragically, all humans are on a battlefield where a tremendous war is being played out. That war entails the hatred of Satan against all humanity versus the love of God for them. This is the fundamental reason why there are doctrines of demons. Satan's purpose for spreading falsehoods is not just for the sake of being evil. Nor is it to momentarily deceive or mislead. Satan's eye is on a bigger trophy—the souls of the unsaved.

When we perceive God's judgment as being too harsh, we dismiss what sin does to humanity, and what it did to the Son of God.

The information you've read thus far may not be new to you, but perhaps you haven't connected it to demonic doctrines in action. That is exactly the point. Satan spreads his doctrines in ways that don't call attention to their origin. Regardless of the level of your awareness, I know that you have felt the force of demonic doctrines in opposition to your desire to live according to God's Word. I have felt it too, and I

---

know these doctrines can feel oppressive, but I want to encourage you to use this force to your advantage.

FACE INTO THE WIND

I love airplanes, and for that matter, anything that flies. From my earliest years, I have been fascinated with flight and the sensation that flying provides. When I was young, I would do everything possible to go to an airport near where I lived in Orange County, California. It was a sweet little airfield called Meadowlark Airport, situated about a mile from the shore of the Pacific. In my mind, it was a perfect place. I loved riding my bike to Meadowlark and parking in the tall grass, ready for a day of observing the miracle of flight.

Sitting next to the runway, I consistently saw the pilots do something I thought was strange. When they took off, they made sure that their Cessna 150 or twin-engine Commander headed into the wind. In the afternoon, that almost always meant they were heading toward the Pacific with strong breezes coming onshore. The fact that the pilots would throttle up and take off into the wind seemed absolutely backward to me. I thought, *Wouldn't it be easier to go with the wind and have it push you so that you could take off faster?* But not only was I wrong, I was dead wrong. For a plane to fly, it must get into the wind. It must grab the air around it to generate resistance against its wings. There must be positive and negative pressure to help generate lift. The greater the opposition, the greater the lift. This was one of my earliest lessons in how opposition can be used for good.

> God's love is strong enough to take you through the hardest trials and the toughest temptations.

Like the onshore winds, Satan's opposition to the kingdom of God will change direction, but unlike the winds, it will never stop. Thankfully, God has given us the means to turn into the wind and rise above

Satan's schemes: perfect love. First John 4:18 tells us that "perfect love casts out fear." Greater than any force coming against us is the perfect love of God for us!

In chapter 3, we looked at the importance of testing the spirits, per 1 John 4:1. Did you notice how John began verse 1? He addressed you and me as *beloved*. You need to circle, underline, draw arrows to this word, or do whatever it takes to make it stand out in your Bible. "Beloved" is in your Bible because as God's child, you are dearly loved—designated for His affection and special favor.

Beloved is a term of endearment so full of tender meaning that we humans can scarcely comprehend its fullness. There is nothing quite like it. The incredible depth of God's love for us is beyond our full grasp, but Paul gave us a glimpse of its magnitude when he said,

> Nothing can ever separate us from God's love. Neither death nor life, neither angels nor demons, neither our fears for today nor our worries about tomorrow—not even the powers of hell can separate us from God's love. No power in the sky above or in the earth below—indeed, nothing in all creation will ever be able to separate us from the love of God that is revealed in Christ Jesus our Lord (Romans 8:38-39 NLT).

Those verses are mighty in both meaning and application. My friend, God's love is strong enough to take you through the hardest trials and the toughest temptations. It will help you stand your ground when opposition and persecution come your way.

Jude 21 tells believers to "keep yourselves in the love of God." Some could read this verse and mistakenly think they need to do something to keep themselves saved. But Jude's command has nothing to do with salvation. What was Jude saying? We are eternally secure in the love of Christ and kept by the power of it. But like any love relationship, we need to maintain and nurture it.

Those who depart from Christ depart from the love of God. Those who reject the commands of Jesus reject His love. Jesus made this connection in John 15:9-11: "As the Father loved Me, I also have loved you; abide in My love. If you keep My commandments, you will abide in My love, just as I have kept My Father's commandments and abide in His love."

Keeping yourself and abiding both flow from a relationship with Jesus Christ. Believer, get alone with God, just you and Him. Read His love letter to you—the Bible. It's there that He will show you His character and ways. His promises will become the love language that fortifies your soul. Then, when the devil offers alternatives, you'll have the strength and knowledge to resist. As Charles Spurgeon says, "Love God, and you will not love false doctrine. Keep the heart of the church right, and her head will not go far wrong; let her abide in the love of Jesus, and she will abide in the truth."[4]

The power and truth of God's love overcomes every lie of Satan, and every doctrine of demons. Keep yourself inside of it, strap in, and get ready for the ride of your life!

CHAPTER 5

DAZED BY DECEPTIONS WITHIN THE CHURCH

In my estimation, there wasn't a better place than Southern California to grow up in during the 1960s and 1970s. It was the place to be. We had outdoor amusements like snow skiing in winter and summers filled with sun, sand, and surf. If that weren't enough, we could camp or hike in the Mojave Desert. The sheer beauty of the many different landscapes so close together was special. California's geographical settings are unlike those of any other state in America, and possibly the entire world. Yet all these natural entertainments didn't seem to be enough to keep people happy.

The thrills of California's outdoors eventually gave way to the amusements of manufactured sensations and computer-generated simulation. Walt Disney's dream of creating a place where kids could play and enjoy themselves was joined by Knott's Berry Farm, Marine Land, Sea World, and Magic Mountain. Rather than the splendor of God's creation, man's inventions grabbed our attention. Today, as we observe what is happening within the church, we can easily see a similar phenomenon. In spite of the profound beauty of the church and Jesus Christ's sovereign act of atonement on its behalf, believers are turning away from the church and seeking fulfillment elsewhere.

At the cross, Christ paid the penalty for our sin, erasing our incalculable offenses against the righteousness of God. And if that weren't enough, His resurrection from the dead provided justification for all who will believe in Him. And unlike what this world can offer, the gospel message is enough—and it is powerful! So powerful that it exploded out from Jerusalem, Judea, and Samaria to the ends of the earth and down through the ages until it reached your ears and mine. The apostle Paul said that the gospel is "the power of God to salvation" (Romans 1:16). There isn't a more beautiful message in all the world.

> The Lord never strives to be relevant to the culture.

The manufactured amusements of Disney's Magic Kingdom, and other places like it, can never compare with the glory of God's creation. Similarly, there are those who have attempted to create a Christianity of their own liking but have failed epically. But that has not stopped these apostates from giving it a try. Sadly, for such people, the gospel is not enough.

AMUSING THE CHURCH TO DEATH

There is often confusion among Christians about the difference between a backslider and an apostate. The Bible clearly says that it is impossible to lose your salvation, but if you're not careful, you can allow your love for Christ to grow cold and backslide into old ways. To that person, the Lord says, "Repent, and I will forgive" (see Hosea 14:4; Revelation 2:5). An apostate is altogether different. Apostates never experience saving faith. They act like a believer on the outside but inwardly remain in a state of unbelief (Luke 8:13). Scripture teaches that some will even perform miracles, but in the end, they will depart from identifying with Jesus Christ because they were never born again (Matthew 7:22-23). First John 2:19 says, "They were not of us; for if they had been of us, they would have continued with us." And Matthew 7:20 informs us, "By their fruits you will know them."

Second Thessalonians 2:3 warns of an apostasy or "falling away" before Christ's return. This refers to pastors and teachers who marry secular ideologies to Scripture. Jude 12 calls these apostates "clouds without water, carried about by the winds; late autumn trees without fruit, twice dead, pulled up by the roots." They put on a good show but offer no spiritual refreshment, leaving their churches dying from hunger and thirst.

Because apostates operate within churches, it's wise to ask, What defines a church? The Bible says that it must be a New Testament church. And by that, I mean it must adhere to Scripture—both the Old and New Testaments—which I want to emphasize is almost missing in many of today's churches. These churches spend an enormous amount of time and effort conforming themselves to the whims of the day rather than the gospel. What they fail to realize is that God's Word does not need human help, power, nor intervention. The Lord never strives to be relevant to the culture.

The pure, unadulterated gospel message has been taken ahold of and abused by those whose human calling is to amuse. It is being maligned by those who claim to be its friends but are, in fact, not. I want to remind you that the word *gospel* implies repentance, but the issue of sin and call to repentance are the very things apostates feel must be avoided in their messages. They're not entertaining enough. In place of the fruit of repentance, you'll find an epidemic of carnality. They've yielded to the flesh, not the Spirit. I know I am painting with a broad brushstroke here, but I speak with charity. Many of today's churches are best described as being like the church at Laodicea. Read what Jesus said about it in the book of Revelation:

To the angel of the church of the Laodiceans write,

"These things says the Amen, the Faithful and True Witness, the Beginning of the creation of God: 'I know your works, that you are neither cold nor hot. I could wish you were cold or hot. So then, because you are lukewarm, and neither cold nor hot, I will vomit you out of My mouth. Because you say, "I am rich, have become wealthy, and have need of nothing"—and do not know that you are wretched, miserable, poor, blind, and naked—I counsel you to buy from Me gold refined in the fire, that you may be rich; and white garments, that you may be clothed, that the shame of your nakedness may not be revealed; and anoint your eyes with eye salve, that you may see. As many as I love, I rebuke and chasten. Therefore be zealous and repent. Behold, I stand at the door and knock. If anyone hears My voice and opens the door, I will come in to him and dine with him, and he with Me. To him who overcomes I will grant to sit with Me on My throne, as I also overcame and sat down with My Father on His throne.

"'He who has an ear, let him hear what the Spirit says to the churches'" (Revelation 3:14-22).

Jesus' words to the Laodiceans make it plain that they had lost their biblical values, and when you lose your values, you lose your convictions. When you lose your convictions, you will eventually lose your purpose and begin trusting in your effort and self-power. You will voice the same self-sufficient attitude as the Laodiceans: "I am rich, have become wealthy, and have need of nothing."

The Laodiceans had an elevated opinion of themselves. They were the type of people who would say, "Look what we've done. We achieved all this through our superior approach to ministry and the latest and greatest techniques." But the truth is that they had drifted from what was plain and clear in the Scriptures to a more socially acceptable state of easy believism and what I call "churchianity."

Eschatologically, Laodicea is the church of the last days. And as happened at Laodicea, much of what is called Christianity and the church today has little to nothing to do with godliness. I have no doubt that we are living in the Laodicean period today.

REPLACEMENTS IN THE CHURCH
A Different Interpretation

Discernment is sorely lacking but much needed among today's Christians. Once-solid Christian colleges, universities, and seminaries are promoting popular courses that teach the Bible through literary devices. By wrapping their teachings in a winsome and seemingly intellectual style, they cast disparaging shadows across the authority of Scripture. In one such class, the instructor mocked the fact that God condemned the serpent to crawl on his belly, which, in his view, is a silly statement because that's what snakes do. Yet the Bible makes it clear that serpents could stand erect in the garden of Eden—not to mention talk—and its judgment resulted in having to slither. The instructor's insertion of his unfounded opinion introduces the idea that individuals have the liberty to draw their own conclusions from what he calls the Genesis story. And that leads to another problem—Genesis is not a story. Genesis is God's factual account of early history, beginning with creation and moving forward.

How you approach the Bible and with what predisposition or predilection means everything to your beliefs. New ways of interpreting Scripture have led to a new, powerless dynamic in the church. It has pivoted toward a social gospel, a distorted gospel, a woke gospel that is anything but the gospel. *Woke* is a modern term that should never apply to any church because it refers to a progressive political ideology based on perceived social injustices and prejudices regarding race, gender, and sexual orientation—all of which are already addressed in the Bible.

Churches identifying as woke prove that they listen to the world more than the Holy Spirit. How so? The Holy Spirit does not need to be awakened. The Spirit doesn't suddenly wake up to some issue, trend, or narrative He previously overlooked or ignored. He does not need to learn anything because He knows everything. He is eternally relevant.

When a church adopts secular verbiage and ideas and incorporates them into its teachings, it has departed from complete dependence upon God's Word and its authority. Yet many churches that claim to be biblically sound now identify as woke. And like the children of Israel, they have mistakenly left the ancient path set by God. "My people have forgotten Me…they have caused themselves to stumble in their ways, from the ancient paths, to walk in pathways and not on a highway" (Jeremiah 18:15).

The church is being deceived by pastors who have fumbled God's Word. Many in the pulpit not only see Genesis as symbolic poetry but also don't study the prophets and increasingly announce that you don't really need to read the Old Testament. I believe one of the significant marks of a woke church is the avoidance of teaching significant amounts of Old Testament scriptures. Yet without the Old Testament, there is no way for you to fully understand the New Testament. Nor will you be able to identify Jesus as the Messiah. Some even say that the Old Testament no longer applies to believers, which I find interesting because Jesus' words contradict their position. In Matthew 5:17-18, Jesus said, "Do not think that I came to destroy the Law or the Prophets. I did not come to destroy but to fulfill. For assuredly, I say to you, till heaven and earth pass away, one jot or one tittle will by no means pass from the law till all is fulfilled." Jesus came to fulfill every part of the Old Testament, right down to every comma and period.

Second Timothy 3:16 tells us, "All Scripture is given by inspiration of God, and is profitable for doctrine, for reproof, for correction, for instruction in righteousness." Again, I remind you that when the Bible says all, it means all.

You can spot a so-called woke church because it has also cut ties with biblical orthodoxy from both the Old and New Testaments. Its twisted thinking on morality directly contradicts what God has said is good and right. The only outcome possible from such error is moral relativism, which deviates from God's commandments.

The woke church has also exploited the social issues prevalent in our day. As I write this, the American church's response to social and political agendas has deeply shaken its foundation, which isn't bad because this has exposed a vast chasm. On one side sits the woke church, drawn into doctrinal error through emotionally appealing ideas rooted in Marxist ideology. On the other side is Jesus' church, resting upon "the pillar and ground of the truth" (1 Timothy 3:15).

A Different View of Israel

What Satan cannot destroy, he seeks to distort or replace. There is a key component of deception within the church today that is often overlooked or ignored entirely: the idea that the church has replaced Israel.

Replacement theology is known by several names that you may have heard of: covenant theology, fulfillment theology, expansion theology, and restoration theology, among others. Whatever name it goes by, replacement theology has no scriptural basis and ignores the facts. Be that as it may, well-known progressive pastors and seminary professors are substituting the church for Israel in their interpretation of Scripture. While replacement theology is popular today, it has ancient roots. Second-century fringe Christian communities taught that because the Jews rejected Jesus Christ as Messiah at His first coming, God, in turn, rejected them entirely. But that is not correct.

God's promises to the Jewish people are powerful and eternal. Rather than attempting to explain away Israel by replacing it with the church, we should be looking at what the Bible says about the Jewish people's future. God gave ample warning that if Israel rejected His leadership, He would judge them according to their ways (see Deuteronomy 28).

And if they persisted, they would be cast out to the four corners of the earth until the last days. History shows that Israel continued its path of rebellion and was eventually expelled from its land in judgment much like Adam and Eve were cast out of Eden. But the Jews' dispersion does not prove God's rejection of Israel, nor does their rejection of the Messiah. On the contrary, they demonstrate that God held true to His word to chastise His people.

Unfortunately, erroneous biblical interpretation has created a history of atrocities done in the name of Jesus Christ against the Jewish people. There is no doubt that this mistaken thinking has been the route leading to the current Boycott, Divestment, and Sanctions movement (BDS) and antisemitism.

I believe replacement theology also plays right into the hands of the Islamist agenda. The false doctrine of replacement theology and Islam are self-serving bedfellows because both deny the current state of Israel's right to exist. Many Christians who espouse replacement theology also reject prophetic portions of the Old Testament and the veracity of Jesus' promise to fulfill it. Yet, for Jesus to fulfill biblical prophecy, Israel must be back in their land before Christ's second coming, as they are today.

There are many dangers surrounding the fallacies of replacement theology. One major problem is that it inserts the church directly into the seven-year tribulation. To require the church to face God's wrath is to say that there is no blessed hope and glorious appearing of Jesus Christ, or rapture of the church, before the tribulation (see Titus 2:13). Such thinking fails to understanding what God's prophetic Word says about the nation of Israel as clearly announced in Daniel 9:24-27:

> Seventy weeks are determined
> for your people and for your holy city,
> to finish the transgression,
> to make an end of sins,
> to make reconciliation for iniquity,

to bring in everlasting righteousness,
to seal up vision and prophecy,
and to anoint the Most Holy.

Know therefore and understand,
that from the going forth of the command
to restore and build Jerusalem
until Messiah the Prince,
there shall be seven weeks and sixty-two weeks;
the street shall be built again, and the wall,
even in troublesome times.

And after the sixty-two weeks
Messiah shall be cut off, but not for Himself;
and the people of the prince who is to come
shall destroy the city and the sanctuary.
The end of it shall be with a flood,
and till the end of the war desolations are
determined.

Then he shall confirm a covenant with many for one week;
but in the middle of the week
he shall bring an end to sacrifice and offering.
And on the wing of abominations shall be one who
makes desolate,
even until the consummation, which is determined,
is poured out on the desolate.

At first glance, Daniel's 70-weeks prophecy can appear confusing, which is why I highly recommend Sir Robert Anderson's book *The Coming Prince*. Anderson's exacting calculations concerning the book of Daniel's 70-weeks prophecy help us to understand God's prophetic plan for the nation of Israel.

The prophetic time clock for Daniel's prophecy began with King

Artaxerxes Longimanus's command on March 5, 444 BC to restore and rebuild Jerusalem (see Nehemiah 2:1-8; Daniel 9:25). We know from Daniel 9:2 that each one-week period represents seven years, so from the king's decree to the Messiah's time would be 483 years. How can 444 BC to AD 33 equal 483 years? The calculation is based on the Babylonian calendar of 360 days rather than our modern 365-day calendar. The 483 years come to a total of 173,880 days—which brings us to March 30, AD 33—the exact day Jesus rode into Jerusalem on a donkey on Palm Sunday (see Matthew 21:1-9).

Daniel 9:26 also foretold that the Messiah would be cut off for a capital offense (April 6, AD 33). Afterward, Jerusalem and the temple would be destroyed, which they were in AD 70. But this still leaves Israel with one seven-year period of time yet to be fulfilled. The prophetic time clock has been paused until Daniel's final seventh week—the tribulation period—begins. God's promise to the nation of Israel of a future week remains to be fulfilled literally.

Christians and those who want to study Jewish history in its fullest sense must carefully read the entire Bible to see what it says about Israel's creation and destiny. In doing so, they will discover that God is not done with the nation of Israel or the Jewish people.

The prophetic revelations of the Old Testament are so clear that they frustrate those who refuse to believe God's great commitment to Israel in the last days. In fact, hear me clearly on this: If God does not keep His future promises to Israel and the Jewish people, then He has no obligation whatsoever to keep His New Testament promises to you, me, and the church. Allow me to repeat that: If God does not fulfill His promises to Israel, including those of chastisement, you have no assurance that He will keep His promises to you.

A Different Design for Men and Women

God's design for men and women has been the accepted standard since the beginning of time—that is, until two landmark decisions. In

1973, the United States Supreme Court ruled in the case of *Roe v. Wade* that women had the right to abort—to terminate—their unborn children. That same year, the American Psychiatric Association no longer designated homosexuality as a mental disorder, declaring it to be normal behavior. Unrestrained abortion and deviant sexuality, which grew worse during the free-love movement of the 1960s, initiated a chain reaction that gradually reshaped the culture and, in turn, the church. What today's church has come to allow and tolerate, and even embrace, is a clear indication of the insidious nature of this specific deception.

So that we base our thinking on a good foundation, let's first look at God's design.

> God created man in His own image; in the image of God He created him; male and female He created them. Then God blessed them, and God said to them, "Be fruitful and multiply; fill the earth and subdue it; have dominion over the fish of the sea, over the birds of the air, and over every living thing that moves on the earth" (Genesis 1:27-28).

When God announced that He had created humanity in His image, He wasn't saying that we are physical versions of Him. To be created in God's image means that we, of all living creatures, are uniquely designed to mirror His moral likeness. He gave us the ability to think, create, reason, experience, and enjoy things that neither animals nor angels know of. He also made us male and female, and He did it in such a way that we can procreate and fulfill His plan to "be fruitful and multiply" (Genesis 1:28). Scripture leaves no doubt that God desires a husband and a wife to come together to create a family.

The family speaks to us not only of a biological process but also of logic, rationale, and reason. The family unit is one of God's ordained methods for ensuring that His Word and His will permeate society. Malachi 2:15 backs this up: "Did He not make them one, having a remnant of the Spirit? And why one? He seeks godly offspring." Yet the church has moved away from what is necessary for creating strong, healthy, and lasting families. To make my point, how often do you hear pastors counter the subversive form of masculinity that is infiltrating their congregations?

The declining number of strong, godly men in the church is alarming. I believe that God's principles for biblical masculinity should be proclaimed from every pulpit. And when it's not, it's up to men to pick up their Bibles and discover what it means to be men like Joshua, David, and Daniel. But the investigation shouldn't stop there. Grotesque manifestations of manhood, such as seen in Ahab, Manasseh, and Nabal, must be avoided, but we can also learn a great deal by studying them.

We would also do well to learn from the strong masculinity of Jesus Christ Himself. Jesus was God in human skin, but He was also a man's man. Yes, you heard me correctly. He acted like a man, spoke like one, and modeled manhood for us. A man who models himself after Jesus will be a servant leader. Jesus fed hungry crowds, rebuked religious hypocrites, comforted the brokenhearted and downcast, and washed His disciples' feet. Nothing was beneath Him. Biblical masculinity means being a man of strength and sensitivity, firm yet tender. When the church teaches and nurtures biblical masculinity, it honors the Word of God.

Biblical Masculinity

Biblical masculinity is what the church and, by extension, the world needs today. I don't want to take jabs at how Christian men try to fit in with the culture by how they dress, live, and act. But I will say that a Christian man ought to look the part and be the part rather than get caught up in worldliness that lends itself to the castration of manhood. That may sound too strong for some readers, but just ten minutes of watching television commercials will tell you that I am correct in making this observation.

Compared to the role models of previous generations, the media portrays men as bumbling fools. Apparently, we don't know how to lead a family, make decisions, or even get groceries properly. We are even seeing men be left out of the picture entirely. Instead, two women are raising the children, with no dad or husband present. Commercials aren't the only place this new norm is played out. Sitcoms and movies cast women as dominant alpha types with male sidekicks who lack the traits typically associated with manhood. These types of role reversals and ways of thinking have crept into the church with little resistance. Satan has been gaining surrendered territory.

How does biblical masculinity look different from what is currently called manhood? I am going to frame this in the context of married men, but even if you're a single guy, listen up. Store this information for future use, and I promise you will be blessed.

According to the Bible, a man should love his family. Loving your wife means setting aside your selfishness and any destructive personal issues. All men carry some baggage from the past—sometimes, it's more like luggage. But we must constantly fight against those struggles so they don't destroy our marital or family relationships. We must seek God's will and His design for manhood so we can be the husband and father our family needs.

In Ephesians 5, we read about the husband's responsibility to love his wife as Christ loves the church. Men have told me they are intimidated by the language of verse 26, which describes how Christ sanctifies His church by washing her through His Word. Husbands often assume that this means they must do an in-depth Bible study with their wife. They wind up overthinking God's command and give up before they even get started. Don't let that happen! Grab your Bible, get together with your wife, and begin with the first chapter of a short book like Philippians. Set it up so that you read verse 1 aloud to your wife, she reads verse 2 aloud to you, and then you follow with verse 3. When you're done reading the chapter, close your Bibles and pray for one another based on what you've just read. Time together in the Word can be that simple.

Biblical Femininity

We cannot leave the biblical model for men without talking about women. In the United States, we recently confirmed a female Supreme Court justice who, when asked to define a woman, replied, "I'm not a biologist." I will not comment on her vacuous answer except to say it is a sad day when a woman cannot or will not define what she is. We can be thankful that God's Word is not confused nor woke when it comes to womanhood.

According to Genesis 2:20, no worthy or suitable companion was found for Adam, so God put him into a deep sleep and took one of his ribs to create Eve. The science behind this is fantastic, but from a devotional standpoint, the rib is closest to man's heart. This speaks of God's tenderness regarding Eve and her descendants, and therefore, women should be treated in the same manner. In Christianity, God calls for women to be honored and held in high esteem, in contrast to pagan religions that degrade, abuse, and suppress women.

That God made men and women differently is not a comment on their value before Him—both are of equal worth.

Women are very capable of excelling in government, academia, law enforcement, business, and more. I applaud the use of their God-given talents in whatever field they enter, but that doesn't mean we should overlook the distinct differences between men and women and how God wants to use them. I may be oversimplifying when I say this, but I think you will understand when I say that generally speaking, men can struggle with inattentiveness. And women are apt to be more tender, diplomatic, and persuasive. Neither of those observations means that women can't be firm and men can't be attentive. But we must ask: Have we allowed ourselves to be conditioned by sociology classes, media, and other mediums to accept unbiblical models of manhood and womanhood?

By God's design, a woman is gifted in ways that a man is not, and vice versa. God intends for men and women to complement and strengthen one another. Today's church should take the lead by showing boys how to be boys and girls how to be girls. We shouldn't delegate that task to the world. The newer generations need to see the fundamental but beautiful differences between a man and a woman, a husband and a wife, and a father and a mother.

Unfortunately, the church's silence on these matters is deafening. If we want to take back our young people, we must speak up. There is too much at stake to keep silent. The health and stability of future generations depends on it.

We've just looked at several significant ways the church has become something other than what God called it to be. Deceived by unbiblical theology and ruled by emotion, the church has become bruised, battered, and weakened by its affiliation with the world. It is no longer the standard of righteousness or salt and light that it once was. Of course, Satan is behind it all. He knows that persecution causes the church to go deeper and grow stronger, so he has accomplished his dirty work through deception. Satan has lulled believers into a spiritual stupor. He has dazed their hearts and minds.

RAISE THE WARNING FLAG

The daze in which we live poses a danger for unsuspecting Christians, not unlike the illustration famous preacher H.A. Ironside used in his book *Illustrations of Bible Truth* involving two trains traveling on the same track. One train held children on their way home from school, and the other freight. The train carrying the children broke down on the tracks, and the engineer dispatched a flagman to go back a distance and warn the coming freight train. The flagman went to his position and raised the warning flag. The freight train barreled by, blew its horn as a signal of understanding, yet kept going. As it rounded a blind bend, it collided with the passenger cars, killing everyone except the freight train's engineer, who leaped to safety.

Days later, the engineer and flagman were ordered into court to give an account. The judge asked, "Why didn't you stop when you saw the flag?" The engineer replied, "I wasn't supposed to stop." But the flagman affirmed he had held up a red flag. The judge then questioned the engineer. "What does red mean to you?" He said, "Red means 'stop' to me, but he didn't hold up a red flag. He held up a yellow flag. Yellow means caution, so I began preparing myself but couldn't see anything urgent."

> God has purposefully placed you and me in this moment of history.

An argument broke out about the color of the flag the engineer saw, and the judge ordered it be brought to the courtroom. The flag was produced, and the flagman held it up. Everyone gasped. It was yellow. The flag was the one he'd always used but didn't inspect. It had once been red, but over the course of time, the sun had bleached it to a faded yellow.[1]

The flagman's failure cost innocents their lives, and I find the parallel to today's pulpit teaching striking. Too many have distorted or watered down the Word of God—conviction has been washed out of it. The gospel is no longer red. It's become a faded yellow, leaving people with no idea of the approaching catastrophe.

As the world races down the track toward the return of Jesus Christ, the urgency for believers to raise the warning flag of biblical truth is great. And like the sons of Issachar, we must understand what we're seeing and know what we ought to do (see 1 Chronicles 12:32).

Our understanding of the times has grown tremendously, but arming ourselves with knowledge is not enough. We must "be dressed for service and keep our lamps burning" (see Luke 12:35 NLT).

In ancient times, a man dressed and ready for service tucked up—girded—his long outer robe into the belt around his waist. This action prepared him to work or fight unhindered. He also made sure that nothing would weigh him down or hold him back (see Hebrews 12:1). Peter had something similar in mind when he said, "Gird up the loins of your mind" (1 Peter 1:13). The New American Standard Bible translates that phrase as "prepare your minds for action." Peter also reminds believers, "He who called you is holy, you also be holy in all your conduct, because it is written, 'Be holy, for I am holy'" (1 Peter 1:15-16). I like that! Christians need an unhindered life and tough-minded holiness if they're going to be ready to work and fight for the truth.

Those who understand the times know that night is coming. We can sense it, it's palatable. We see it in the darkness enveloping the world and the church. Before electricity, oil lamps were essential for light, and before darkness fell, you needed to have sufficient oil on hand. You had to be prepared. God has purposefully placed you and me in this moment of history. Are you dressed for service? Are you prepared? Are you holding up your lamp so others can see what's going on around them?

My prayer is that we would be strengthened against emotionally based theology. I pray we would revive the lost art of critical thinking and scrutinize everything against the Word of truth, for it alone gives wisdom and clarity. And may we raise the warning flag that runs red with the blood of Christ.

CHAPTER 6

DAZED BY EASY BELIEVISM

O ur culture hates to be uncomfortable. We have whole industries geared toward soothing our senses and making us feel at ease and unruffled. This creates a perfect environment for the deception of an undemanding, easy-to-swallow gospel to take root. Before we approach the topic of easy believism, I want to set the stage by looking briefly at the trichotomy of man.

The Bible teaches that we are body, soul, and spirit (1 Thessalonians 5:23). In the garden of Eden, prior to the fall of Adam and Eve, each of those areas was in their proper order. Adam and Eve's spirits lived uppermost, their soul was subject to the spirit, and the body was subject to both. But with the fall came a reversal of order. Fleshly passions began to take control—now, our bodies are slaves to sin. The Holy Spirit no longer leads the soul. This leaves the soul prompted, tempted, and coerced by the demands of the flesh. And our spirit is in a coma, so to speak, until we come to Jesus Christ.

Life in the garden was perfect, and God gave Adam and Eve the freedom to eat from every tree, with one exception. God forbade them to eat of the tree of the knowledge of good and evil for this reason: "for in the day that you eat of it you shall surely die" (Genesis 2:17). The moment they consumed that fruit, they experienced spiritual death. We know it was spiritual because Genesis records that they continued to live after the fall, but eventually, they died physically as well. Every one of us experiences physical death because of Adam and Eve's sin, but if we are born again, physical death is simply a transition to living in Christ's presence forever.

The gospel is about the reality of an eternal life in heaven and a new life here and now. When we are what Jesus called "born again" (see John 3:3), the spirit is placed uppermost, the soul retains its place in the center, and the flesh takes a lesser seat. That, my friend, is the best news ever! But there is an enemy to this truth, which is mentioned in 1 John 4:3: "Every spirit that does not confess that Jesus Christ has come in the flesh is not of God."

In chapter 3 of this book, we looked at 1 John 4:1-6 regarding testing the spirits. In case you didn't notice it, the word "spirit" is not capitalized as it is when Scripture refers to the Holy Spirit. This is a lesser spirit. The spirit John refers to is undoubtedly human, but not led by God's Spirit. There is a demonic force driving it.

ENEMIES OF THE GOSPEL

With the eternal destination of every person outside of Christ at stake, a determined battle is being waged over what constitutes the gospel. Enemies of the gospel replace the biblical gospel with an easy believism message, and they are everywhere. Beginning in Matthew 13:24, Jesus taught three parables that expose the presence of these influencers in every church and every work of God. Let's take a look at what He said:

> The kingdom of heaven is like a man who sowed good seed in
> his field; but while men slept, his enemy came and sowed tares
> among the wheat and went his way. But when the grain had

sprouted and produced a crop, then the tares also appeared. So the servants of the owner came and said to him, "Sir, did you not sow good seed in your field? How then does it have tares?" He said to them, "An enemy has done this." The servants said to him, "Do you want us then to go and gather them up?" But he said, "No, lest while you gather up the tares you also uproot the wheat with them. Let both grow together until the harvest, and at the time of harvest I will say to the reapers, 'First gather together the tares and bind them in bundles to burn them, but gather the wheat into my barn'" (Matthew 13:24-30).

Next, Jesus gave a parable concerning a mustard seed:

The kingdom of heaven is like a mustard seed, which a man took and sowed in his field, which indeed is the least of all the seeds; but when it is grown it is greater than the herbs and becomes a tree, so that the birds of the air come and nest in its branches (Matthew 13:31-32).

And the last of the three parables is this:

The kingdom of heaven is like leaven, which a woman took and hid in three measures of meal till it was all leavened (Matthew 13:33).

What do we learn from tares, mustard seeds, and leaven as they relate to the work of God on Earth? First, we understand that tares are among us and resemble us, but the similarities end there. The enemy, Satan, has sown false teachers and their false converts in his attempt to destroy Christ's work. What's interesting about tares is that they contain a toxin that causes sickness and can destroy the harvest. So why wait until the very end to separate the good from the bad? Why not get rid of them now? The implication of an end-time harvest tells us that a future judgment is coming. God Himself will remove them. Jesus said to let the tares go because their judgment on that day will be thorough, while His people will be kept safe.

Next, we see that the mustard seed experienced an abnormal growth that allowed birds to lodge in its branches. When Scripture mentions birds, it is often in a good way. Take, for instance, when Jesus said that a sparrow cannot fall to the ground without the Father knowing about it (Matthew 10:29). In that context, birds are good. But the birds flocking to this strange tree-like plant are not good. In this parable, the birds of the air have an evil connotation. The same applies to the leaven hidden in the meal. In biblical typology, leaven always refers to sin.

> Even though your Bible is thousands of years old, it is never out of date.

What is Jesus telling us? The church will grow to such a size that enemies of the gospel will infiltrate and infuse it with destructive doctrines. I know that sounds ominous, but be encouraged. Their judgment is not idle. Ultimately, none of them will get away with what they are doing.

Enemies Teach a Modernized Gospel

Easy believism is rooted in the conscious or unconscious neglect of the whole counsel of God's Word and requires alterations to the gospel found in the Bible. Today, churches are quickly succumbing to this alternative plan of salvation lest they upset anyone.

Listen: Even though your Bible is thousands of years old, it is never out of date. The gospel message never needs updating. But if you listen to the modernized gospel of today, you will hear a version based on current wisdom, the political tide, and what feels emotionally correct. At the same time, have you noticed how traditional wisdom, as we once knew it, has gone by the wayside? People now rely on weird perversions of truth in their slippery slide away from biblical wisdom and common-sense logic. And this has influenced the church.

Far from the Christ-centered gospel is the felt-needs message flooding the church. Colorful flyers and catchy announcements mask the deception behind invitations, such as "Come visit us as we go through 12 steps to having a meaningful life," or "Join us and discover the 5 principles for successful living." Those sound nice, but are they the gospel? Is the first step of the 12 that you must be born again? Does one of the principles deal with your sins? Unfortunately, too many people would rather have 5 principles and 12 steps instead of adhering to what Jesus taught.

There is nothing wrong with principles and steps except that they are not the gospel. Sermons that consistently focus on needs over Christ are not much different than what you will hear from a motivational speaker. Yes, you might hear a Bible verse inserted somewhere to make the teaching seem biblical, but it isn't. It is dangerous and completely misleading.

People come away from this type of teaching with false hope. They have been duped into thinking they have a connection with God. They've been told they're on the right path now, and they're on the road to a new beginning. They have their 12-step outline from a so-called sermon, and they head off with a little bit of what they perceive as Christianity. But they are not converted. They are not changed. In many cases, the message has inoculated them against the gospel with a convenient substitute that feels good.

A SERIES OF MINUSES
The Gospel Minus Sin

When the enemy is at work, the gospel message becomes a series of minuses. One of the first places you'll see this is in the subtraction of what Puritan writer Ralph Venning called "the sinfulness of sin." Anytime the gospel is not taught clearly, it softens the nature of mankind's sinfulness. The Bible, on the other hand, is never ambiguous in its estimation of humanity's standing outside of Christ:

> All have sinned and fall short of the glory of God
> (Romans 3:23).

As it is written:
"There is none righteous, no, not one;
> there is none who understands;
> there is none who seeks after God.
> They have all turned aside;
> they have together become unprofitable;
> there is none who does good, no, not one"
(Romans 3:10-12).

If by the one man's offense death reigned through the one,
much more those who receive abundance of grace and of
the gift of righteousness will reign in life through the One,
Jesus Christ (Romans 5:17).

Wow. The moment Adam blew it, sin was passed down through the entire human race. Every human is SIN positive. We are natural-born sinners—we don't even have to try. It's in us. King David said that you and I were conceived in sin (see Psalm 51:5). Does that mean that the conception of a baby is sinful? No, not at all. But when mom and dad got together and a child was conceived, wired within that baby is a rebelliousness that doesn't take long for the parents to discover.

New moms and dads hate to hear that kind of talk. I know they think that their little bundle is innocent and cuter than a button, but he or she is a little sinner. They may not show it yet, but the desire to sin is part of their nature. Those of you who are parents: Do you remember how volatile your toddler was? One minute they're giving you hugs and kisses, and the next they're on the ground throwing a temper tantrum because you told them no in the toy store. What just happened? Sin. Imagine if toddlers had more strength and mobility. Their outbursts would be disastrous. I'm grateful that God delays the development of their motor skills long enough for us to begin shaping and molding their little hearts.

The Gospel Minus Conviction

The next time you listen to a message, be alert to whether its content makes you aware of attitudes or actions that displease God. I say that because preaching that is soft on sin is devoid of conviction. Why is this so important? Because conviction leads people to turn away from sin and pursue holiness. It is problematic when there is never a cause for conviction—none. When people leave a worship service, and all you hear is, "Oh, I just love coming here. I always feel so good when I leave," something is amiss. I'm not putting down that sentiment, but is that the basis for your church attendance? If feeling good is the only fruit you are looking for, why not go to the local bar or somewhere else?

Give people God's Word, and watch the Holy Spirit grab ahold of those verses or passages and send them straight into their heart. The Bible alone has the power to deliver a verdict as to the state of a person's heart. "The word of God is living and powerful, and sharper than any two-edged sword, piercing even to the division of soul and spirit, and of joints and marrow, and is a discerner of the thoughts and intents of the heart" (Hebrews 4:12). The Spirit will bring the soul of that man or woman to the point that they confess, "Oh God, forgive me of this terrible thing I have done. It breaks my heart to know that I have dishonored You."

As a pastor, I am to present the truth and leave the results in God's hands. In his book *Lectures to My Students*, Charles Spurgeon admonished pastors, "No truth is to be kept back."[1] I like that. I believe those who are being touched by God's Word will respond. Now, granted, not every message is going to convict every person. But, if the Lord is speaking, lives will be touched. People will be encouraged, exhorted, instructed, and convicted. And yes, some will reject the same message that others receive. Jesus said, "My sheep hear My voice, and I know them, and they follow Me" (John 10:27).

Are you attending a church where there is no conviction taking place?

I hope not, because it will also be devoid of repentance, and without repentance there is no transformation.

The Gospel Minus Repentance

If there were ever a missing link in the church today, it would be the presentation of the whole gospel as those in the first-century church understood it. So little do we detect or discern it even in the sermons of sincere pastors. Instead, we hear them enticing people to accept Christ, but with messages that kill. How so? In a desire to see souls won to Christ, pastors and evangelists will say, "If you'd like to receive Jesus Christ today as Lord and Savior, please raise your hand or stand to your feet and come forward as the music plays."

Coming forward has absolutely nothing to do with the gospel. We can go so far as to say neither does announcing the fact that Jesus Christ is Lord—God incarnate, who died on the cross for our sins and rose again from the grave. Such a pronouncement falls flat in the light of the gospel presented by Jesus and the apostles. Can you see what is missing? It's the word *repentance*. *Repentance* is the first word of the gospel. And there cannot be good news without first knowing the bad news. We can never appreciate Jesus Christ as Savior unless we first recognize that we need saving.

When Jesus first presented the gospel, His announcement "The kingdom of God is at hand. Repent, and believe in the gospel" (Mark 1:15) was crystal clear to those listening. His invitation to *metanoia*—the Greek word for "repent"—meant change your mind. Change the way you've been thinking about God and how to know Him.

The requirement of repentance before belief had vivid connotations for disciples like Peter, James, and John. When these fishermen were out sailing and heard *metanoia* called out, they understood that it meant they were to make a 180-degree turn of both sail and rudder, and change course. Likewise, God asks us to consider the direction our life is heading, turn around, and leave that life behind.

Pursuing Christ without changing course is impossible. It locks us in an endless cycle of sin and asking for forgiveness, only to repeat the process again and again. True repentance breaks that cycle.

Repentance is missing from preaching for several reasons. One is that many ministers don't hold the same view of sin as God does. Nor do they view salvation as He does. And let's be honest: Talking about repentance doesn't make you popular. If you tell people, "You need to repent of your sins," there is a good chance they won't listen to another word you say. But, as I have already said, the hearer's response is not our responsibility.

It has been said that a gospel message given without the challenge and call to repent is an illegitimate gospel that produces an illegitimate birth. It invites people to start thinking, *Yeah, that sounds like a good deal. I've got my Costco card, my Visa card, and now I can get my Jesus card too.* This appeals to their flesh yet leaves them dead in their trespasses and sins (Ephesians 2:1).

The Gospel Minus Its Power

No church should dilute doctrine in an effort to get people through its doors. It should reach down and pull people up by the Word of God to receive the grace of God. Second Timothy 4:2 commands pastors and teachers, "Preach the word!" Preach the Bible, not a seminar. Give the authoritative Word of God, not a pep talk or feel-good story.

Watered-down easy believism within the church produces, if anything, weak Christians. They might be churchgoers—some of them having attended for decades—but they have no spiritual power. Consequentially, there is no lasting change taking place in their lives. They live a shallow, superficial life that they've labeled "Christianity."

Lack of spiritual power is often tied to a lack of expositional teaching that goes verse by verse through a book of the Bible. Systematic teaching encourages people to eat of God's Word, dissect it, and apply it to their lives. The result is that they grow deeper and stronger in their walk with the Lord.

When your spiritual diet consists of inspiring stories and topical messages, you will not grow as you should. The power of the gospel won't be at work in you as it could be, leaving you to wonder why you lead a defeated Christian life. It is a tragedy and completely unnecessary.

The Gospel Minus the Cross

First Corinthians 1:17 makes it clear that to preach the gospel is to preach the cross. Paul said, "Christ did not send me to baptize, but to preach the gospel, not with wisdom of words, lest the cross of Christ should be made of no effect."

The most dangerous aspect of easy believism is its devaluation of the cross, the centerpiece of Christianity. When the Bible talks about the cross, it is not referring to a shiny ornamental crucifix on an altar or a piece of jewelry. Such types of physical displays have no power in and of themselves. The power is in the message they represent. The cross is the only means by which you and I gain eternity, which makes it easy to see why Satan attacks it so vigorously.

The power of the cross changes everything!

So-called gospel presentations often come wrapped in the latest trends with entertaining props, but conspicuously absent are truths about the cross. After all, who wants to hear about something so rugged, bloody, and altogether hideous? Yet, when preached rightly and literally, the cross brings men, women, and young girls and boys to the point of salvation. It is "the power of God to salvation for everyone who believes" (Romans 1:16).

Christian, you must understand the absolute necessity of Christ's blood-stained cross—without it, remission of sins is impossible. Jesus Christ, and Him crucified, is the sole basis of our justification before God Almighty.

In John 3:14-15, Jesus said of Himself, "As Moses lifted up the serpent

in the wilderness, even so must the Son of Man be lifted up, that whoever believes in Him should not perish but have eternal life." Just as the
children of Israel, wandering in the wilderness, could not save themselves
from fiery serpents, we, too, cannot save ourselves from the condemnation that our rebelliousness deserves. Only by looking to the cross are
our sins forgiven and heaven secured.

You cannot hide from or sidestep the cross of Christ. You can only
accept or reject it, but once accepted and applied, the power of the cross
changes everything!

ENEMIES OF THE CROSS

Paul warned us about those who dismiss the necessity of embracing
the cross when he said, "For many walk, of whom I have told you often,
and now tell you even weeping, that they are the enemies of the cross
of Christ" (Philippians 3:18). Isn't this amazing? Paul didn't say enemies
of the love of God, baptism, or communion. He singled out enemies of
the cross. To be an enemy of the cross is to reject the cost that it entails.
Again, I quote Charles Spurgeon, who said to do this is to make the
cross "a very small affair."[2]

Easy believism degrades the cross by suggesting it is possible to come
to Christ without actually following Christ. This is a well-worn trap of
Satan. It goes like this: You've been praying for the salvation of a friend
for months, maybe even years. You finally get your friend into church,
and you're sitting there thinking, *I wish the pastor would say this or that.
I want him to say whatever it takes to get my friend saved!* You want your
friend to respond to Christ so badly that you are hoping that the pastor soft-pedals the gospel.

Can you see how easily this line of thinking can slip off course? You'd
better believe that Satan knows it. He is sitting right next to your friend,
whispering in their ear, "Don't worry, you don't have to give up anything.
You can keep your lusts, lying, and cheating. You can keep your questionable business practices. In fact, your life can continue as it always

has." But what every non-Christian needs to hear is what Jesus said: "If anyone desires to come after Me, let him deny himself, and take up his cross, and follow Me. For whoever desires to save his life will lose it, but whoever loses his life for My sake will find it. For what profit is it to a man if he gains the whole world, and loses his own soul? Or what will a man give in exchange for his soul?" (Matthew 16:24-26).

Unbelievers know how they've been committed to living by the world's standards and lifestyles. They're also aware of the sin hidden deep inside their hearts. The Holy Spirit has been convicting them ever since they could discern between right and wrong. They need to hear that their sins can be erased through what Jesus did at the cross. But if they choose to protect and hang on to the life they're currently living, they'll lose it in the end. My friend, we need to tell them the whole truth, and nothing but the truth! And God will empower us to do exactly that.

How many times have you felt the Holy Spirit prompting you to speak in a loving but direct manner and tell someone the hard truth about their sin? You wanted to tell them about Jesus, but there was a war going on inside. As much as you'd hate to admit it, you didn't want to look like a fool or feel uncomfortable. You became ashamed of the gospel at that moment, making the cross "a very small affair." And boy, does that hurt.

Instead of merely patting people on the back and asking, "Can I pray for you?," plead with them and say, "My friend, I am begging you, please come to Jesus. Don't die without Him. There is no purgatory or second chance. You'll go straight to hell, and it will be your choice. Don't do that! Jesus Christ paid your sin debt; agree with God and repent. He loves you! Come to Him now!"

Once the necessity of the cross is watered down or removed, it is easy to downplay the cost of following Christ. There is no need to talk about how Jesus' death and resurrection should apply to people's daily lives. Ironically, the world is filled with cults that demand 110 percent from their devotees.

The Jehovah's Witnesses group demands that their followers spend hours studying the Bible. These sincere people know more passages than most Christians. I wish that believers knew the Bible like they do. The problem is that Jehovah's Witnesses don't study it accurately or in its context. As a result, their false teachings keep people hell bound.

Or have you ever heard about Indian guru Bhagwan Shree Rajneesh? He became famous in the early 1980s for establishing a large religious commune in Oregon. Thousands lined up to hear his teachings based on a blend of Eastern religion and pop psychology. A good portion of his followers were professional, highly educated people—doctors, professors, and attorneys—who worked 12 hours a day on the commune. Many of these same people sold all their material possessions to give to the cause. Interestingly, at one point, Rajneesh owned 93 Rolls Royce automobiles! Yet his followers remained dutifully committed even after he was deported to India for fraud. Rajneesh is long dead, but you can count on the fact that others have already taken his place.

How is it that people freely submit to the demands of cults, and yet Christians struggle to remain steadfast in their commitment to the One who died for them? Could it be that they've been deceived by the lie of no-cost, no-cross Christianity?

WITNESSES OF THE CROSS

The reality of the cross in our lives is observed by those around us, including our foes. One of the most effective forms of evangelism occurs under the watchful eyes of an unbelieving world. They know we are followers of Jesus, and they are watching us in our day-to-day circumstances, in life's struggles and victories. There is a quote that has been attributed to a couple different people, but it doesn't matter who said it. The last sentence says it all: "Preach the gospel always. And if you must, use words." Isn't that a great challenge?

Our lives ought to be a living billboard, a sign and testimony of the presence of Christ—a beautiful display of His lordship and control.

The ministry of disciple-making occurs as we are yielded vessels for the advancement of God's kingdom. But for this to happen, there must be a starting point of discipleship as seen in Jesus' commissioning of the church in Matthew 28:19.

Jesus told His followers, in what has been called the Great Commission, to go out into all the world, preach the gospel, and make disciples of all nations. The primary work of the church is to make the gospel known with one specific motive: to make disciples.

> When we realize the expense God paid in forgiving our sins, we are immediately humbled by the power of such a display of love.

The Great Commission is for every believer. In fact, I will be so bold as to say that if you're not a follower of Jesus Christ, you will have no passion, desire, or stomach to share about Him. It's not even on your radar because you cannot give away what you don't have. But conversely, if Jesus Christ is in your life, you will make yourself available when God brings the opportunity. Why is this true? Because being a disciple involves disciple-making. It is a fundamental ministry of the Christian life. Disciples reproduce disciples just as birds reproduce birds and sheep reproduce sheep.

The question is, Are you a faithful follower of Jesus? If so, the natural outflow of your life will affect others.

In his Christian classic *The Cost of Discipleship*, Dietrich Bonhoeffer writes that we are saved by the grace of God, and when we act upon that grace in faith, He brings us into His family. But, warns Bonhoeffer, though that grace may be free to us, it cost God everything. It may be free, but it's anything but cheap. There is no such thing as cheap grace, which is an illusory invention of progressive, liberal Christianity, which is a false Christianity.

When we realize the expense God paid in forgiving our sins, we are immediately humbled by the power of such a display of love. We are brought to a place of bowing the heart and bending the knee before Almighty God, who relegated Himself to become like us—human. Born in Bethlehem, according to the Scriptures, He bore the brunt and shame of associating with mankind, only to be betrayed, crucified, buried, and resurrected from the dead. That God's extravagance should be reciprocated with love and devotion should not surprise anyone.

What is the cost of this kind of discipleship? It is the cross, plain and simple. As a disciple of Jesus Christ, picking up your cross and following Him will involve denying your flesh, and that is costly. The cross comes at a cost to your pride and self-will. God designed it that way. He uses the ugly and difficult things in our lives as instruments of growth toward Christlikeness, which, in turn, clearly display the gospel's transforming power.

I know that God has my best interests in mind. His ways have always proven to be excellent and far exceed mine. The reality of the cross in my life means purposing to do His will above my own throughout the day. I can do this only as I apply the Word of God to every situation. When someone disagrees with me, it's okay. Or, when someone has a better idea than I do, that's fine. I no longer have skin in the game, but only God's interest and what is best for His kingdom. In my marriage, picking up my cross is to seek my wife's happiness. I ask the Lord, "How can I be a witness to her in this situation? I know what I want to do. I know what I think I should do. But, Lord, what is it that You would have me to do?"

The way of the cross is not easy, but it is an incredibly liberating way to live. Choosing to pick up your cross becomes a joy when God's Spirit rules and reigns in you. "Now the Lord is the Spirit; and where the Spirit of the Lord is, there is liberty" (2 Corinthians 3:17).

CHAPTER 7

DAZED BY THE DECEPTIVE CRY FOR UNITY

M odern songs such as John Lennon's "Imagine" often hit the top of music charts with their dream of a world uniting in one accord. This desire for unity in our fractured world seems attainable, but is it really? How could anyone think otherwise? After all, aren't we all part of one big family? That depends on your viewpoint. Doesn't the Bible say unity is a good thing? Yes, it does. "Behold, how good and how pleasant it is for brethren to dwell together in unity" (Psalm 133:1).

Unity, as the psalmist describes it, is wonderful. But notice the qualifying word—"brethren." Those of us who are of the household of faith are to dwell together in unity. This is not optional. It is a call to obedience. We are to strive, endeavor, and work hard at keeping the unity of the faith. As brothers and sisters in Christ, our wills and emotions should not take preeminence over our consideration for others. Yet they often do, and strife is the result. It's a rough road when a family doesn't get along, which is why we are supposed to live and walk in the Spirit.

Oneness of mind, heart, and purpose is how the early church survived and thrived. But do not be deceived. The unity you hear clamored for in many places today is altogether different and originates from a dark source. Spiritual entities have dimmed the lights, so to speak, to camouflage their agenda.

THE DECEPTIVENESS OF ECUMENICAL UNITY

We cannot afford to be careless about who we join hands with. Believers are commanded, "If it is possible, as much as depends on you, live peaceably with all men" (Romans 12:18). Christians should aim to live peaceably with everyone—believers and unbelievers alike—but not at the expense of the integrity of biblical doctrine. We must exercise extreme caution because some calls for unity will tug at our emotions yet have no biblical basis.

Christians have been programmed to believe division is wrong. It is easy to see why people buy into the growing movement toward ecumenism, which emphasizes unity among different Protestant denominations, as well as with Catholicism. Joining together despite our differences sounds noble, but the idea that it is okay for you to hold one view while someone else holds to another will depend on the issue at stake.

Christians can and do disagree on things like baptism—immersion versus sprinkling—and whether some spiritual gifts are still valid in today's church. But we are not free to disagree on the essentials that define Christianity:

> The entire Bible is inerrant (Psalm 119:160; 2 Peter 1:21)
>
> There is only one God (Isaiah 43:10)
>
> God is triune, as expressed by the Father, Son, and Holy Spirit (Matthew 28:19)
>
> Salvation is necessary because of humanity's sinful state (Romans 3:23)

Salvation comes through Christ alone (Acts 4:12)

Salvation comes apart from works, through grace alone (Ephesians 2:8-9)

Christ is God (John 10:30)

Christ died, was buried, and rose again (1 Corinthians 15:3-5)

Christ will return to Earth physically at His second coming (Acts 1:11; Revelation 19:11-16)

We shouldn't be against denominations per se if they hold fast to scriptural doctrines. The problem with an ecumenical union is that it forces the participants to refuse to embrace the entirety of the Bible and its essential doctrines.

Your Bible may have the name Tyndale or Wycliffe on the cover, and you might not be aware of the significance of that. As late as the 1600s, the predominant thinking was that only the clergy or priests should read the Bible. But William Tyndale, John Wycliffe, and others like them believed that the common people should have their own Bibles. They dedicated their lives—some unto death—to secure that right. Instead of having a priest or religious figure read select passages and tell people what to believe, they wanted everyone to read the Scriptures for themselves.

Why do I bring this to your attention? There is a history behind the fact you have your own copy of God's Word today. Make use of your Bible and take the time to understand what it says. Unless you read books of the Bible like Romans and Hebrews from start to finish, you will not recognize the similarities and differences between Protestant denominations. Nor will you grasp the significant doctrinal differences between Protestantism and Catholicism, not to mention aberrant "Christian" cults.

Perhaps the most vocal call for unity is coming from the world. People everywhere are appealing for all religious groups—Christian and non-Christian alike—to unite. The ecumenical movement has gone global in its pursuit of unity among all faiths. It seems as if every new crisis or catastrophe comes with another round of cries for religions to unify. If you believe current press releases, ecumenical unity is a worthwhile pursuit that would solve many, if not all, of the world's problems. Not only is that thinking delusional, but it is also demonic in origin.

The desire for unity among different religious groups is longstanding, as a 2019 article from the United States Institute of Peace shows:

> Pope Francis' recent sojourn in the Arabian Peninsula was a powerful symbolic advance for interfaith dialogue: the first visit by a Roman Catholic pontiff to the original homeland of the Islamic faith. Francis joined eminent Muslim, Jewish and other Christian clerics in an appeal for the communal coexistence so desperately needed by a world suffering violence and persecution across humanity's religious divides. The visit's moving imagery included Christians and Muslims together attending the first papal mass on the peninsula. Yet this powerful symbolism will have real impact only if it inspires us all to take concrete steps—notably by governments, educational institutions and faith-based organizations.[1]

Did you notice how the writer used phrases like "moving imagery" and "powerful symbolism" to play on readers' emotions? The article painted a picture reinforcing the idea that it is time for Muslims, Christians, and Jews to come together. A discerning reader should ask, "Is this important? Did God say this is what He wants?" The answer is no to both. The next question should be, "Is this even possible?" Not according to the Bible. Why, then, are we hearing the call for unity among the world's three major religions? Because mankind deems it necessary. But when we hear such pleas, you and I are immediately confronted with a decision. Will we concede to an emotionally based theology, or will we stand on a scriptural one?

Calls to ecumenism tend to rally around social issues that people relate to and support. The Catholic Church is famous for using this tactic to support efforts toward ecumenical union. Pope Francis used Russia's war with Ukraine to call for unity ahead of a meeting with Sunni Islam's Grand Imam in Bahrain. During a trip aimed at bridging the gap between faiths, the pope warned that the world is on the edge of a "delicate precipice" buffeted by "winds of war."[2] We all detest the horrors of war, but can you see how, once again, descriptive language is being used to sway your thinking?

This tactic was also behind the attention-grabbing headline of the November 2022 post from *Watt's Up with That*: "Climate Religion: Egypt's Mount Sinai to receive 'Climate Justice Ten Commandments' during UN summit—Interfaith 'Climate Repentance Ceremonies.'" The world cares about peace and climate change, which makes these appeals tempting. But believers need to wise up to the spirit behind this agenda.

The desire for religious unity is also prevalent in our communities. Over the years, I have received countless invitations to participate in local ecumenical gatherings. One specifically comes to mind. I was asked to participate in a discussion about when Christ would return. I declined the invitation, and later read in the local newspaper that Muslims, Buddhists, Christians, and Mormons were in attendance. Some of them said Christ had already come. Others said no, no, this other event must happen first. Interestingly, the basis for coming together was the idea that a belief in the Messiah's return is supposed to unify those of different faiths. How is unity possible when people from varied religious backgrounds can't agree on something so basic?

The article went on to talk about how we need to focus on beliefs and views we have in common and let go of anything we disagree on. You, too, have heard this sentiment voiced. But frankly, the issues that we disagree on are frequently the most important because they are absolute and mean the difference between adherence to truth or compromise.

Can you imagine Jesus showing up at an ecumenical conference today? What if He walked in and posed the same question that He asked the disciples: "Who do you say that I am?"? You would probably hear answers like, "You are a Bodhisattva, an enlightened one," or "You are the son of Joseph and Mary." Another would say, "You are a descendant of Adam." And undoubtedly, someone in the group would deny Jesus' deity: "You think you're the Son of God, but really, you're only a powerful man." What would these people do with Jesus? It is hard to say. Some might emotionally demand that He recant His claims, but it's more likely that they would gut Him of His deity, deny all the essential doctrines about Him, and embrace Him as a guru. All in the name of unity.

WHY UNITY ISN'T POSSIBLE
You Have a New Family

It's not only what Christians believe that rules out the possibility of uniting with other faiths, it's what they have that others don't. First John 4:4 says, "You are of God, little children, and have overcome them, because He who is in you is greater than he who is in the world."

"You are of God"—those four words speak volumes. First and foremost, this statement implies a birth has occurred. The primary meaning of the Greek word *ek*, translated "of" in your Bible, is "out from." It refers to an object that was inside another and is now separated from it—like a child at birth. A child originates in the womb of its mother. It dwells there as it grows until the day that child comes forth into the world. Likewise, our spiritual life originated with God. There was a day when you were not of God, but when you heard the truth, that truth set you free! You were born again and brought into an intimate relationship as His child.

The reality of being "of God" is that you've been birthed into a new family. You have a new relationship with God the Father, and you have many new brothers and sisters. I have found in my life—perhaps you have noticed this as well—that these relationships often go beyond anything experienced in our natural-born families. The spiritual family you and I are now a part of is powerful and transcends any bloodline in this world. You have heard the saying, "Blood is thicker than water," and scientifically, it's true. Blood has a greater viscosity than water. But if blood is thicker than water, then the Spirit is thicker than blood.

In 1 John 4:4, we read, "He who is in you is greater than he who is in the world." "He who...is greater" is a reference to the Holy Spirit dwelling within you. Because you're now a part of God's family, the Father has fulfilled the Son's promise that He would send the Holy Spirit to live in you.

> I will pray the Father, and He will give you another Helper, that He may abide with you forever—the Spirit of truth, whom the world cannot receive, because it neither sees Him nor knows Him; but you know Him, for He dwells with you and will be in you. I will not leave you orphans; I will come to you (John 14:16-18).

> I tell you the truth. It is to your advantage that I go away; for if I do not go away, the Helper will not come to you; but if I depart, I will send Him to you (John 16:7).

> When He, the Spirit of truth, has come, He will guide you into all truth; for He will not speak on His own authority, but whatever He hears He will speak; and He will tell you things to come (John 16:13).

Now, when opportunities come your way to unite yourself with religious groups or worldly organizations, the Spirit of Truth will warn you not to do that. It is as if God placed a discern-o-meter within His children. I mentioned that term once to my congregation and they laughed, but it is true.

As members of a spiritual family, we rally around God's Word. Its truths dictate our thinking, words, and how we relate to those outside of God's family. We aren't supposed to run around saying that this person is of God and that one is not—that truth will eventually manifest itself. How so? The statement "You are of God" means that you confess what people of other religions do not: Jesus Christ is God revealed in human flesh. Those who belong to pagan cults and other religions can't make that statement of faith.

One of the diabolical schemes behind attempts to unite people of different beliefs is to get Christians to overlook the fact that others do not hold to the deity of Jesus. Maybe you've heard someone call Jesus Lord, yet because of their doctrine, they don't believe in Him for salvation. First Corinthians 12:3 says it is impossible for that person to call Him Lord. "No one can say that Jesus is Lord except by the Holy Spirit." You can't have the Holy Spirit in your life unless you have been born again and brought into the family of God (see Romans 8:14).

A Christian says that Jesus is Lord because that is a core doctrine of their faith. God is involved in everything they do throughout the week, not just on Sunday (see Colossians 3:17). If you are of God, He is the originator and the source of your spiritual vitality. You live your life in Him and through Him, as Galatians 2:20 says: "I have been crucified with Christ; it is no longer I who live, but Christ lives in me; and the life which I now live in the flesh I live by faith in the Son of God, who loved me and gave Himself for me." It is mind-boggling to realize that Jesus wants to live His life in us and through us. It is also a sobering truth that should make us more cautious regarding who we link arms with. It's easy to hook a wagon to something. It's another thing to unhook it.

Now, as members of this spiritual family, there is a great division between us and the "them" of 1 John 4:4. The Greek word translated "them" in that verse is graphic. It means those of a baffling or strange wind. It implies that their doctrine is backward in origin—they're cockeyed in their thinking. The Christian's refusal to accept strange doctrines, whether from those claiming to be Christian or those completely outside of Christianity, makes unity impossible. In fact, the opposite is true: Such disagreement creates division, and it often leads others to express animosity toward us.

No one enjoys being disliked by others, and being hated feels even worse. Yet Jesus said that's what we should expect when we follow Him. The world hated Jesus because He testified that its works were evil, which means we will be hated too. "If the world hates you, you know that it hated Me before it hated you. If you were of the world, the world would love its own. Yet because you are not of the world, but I chose you out of the world, therefore the world hates you" (John 15:18-19).

There is an undeniable rift between those who are of the world and those who are of God. The world loves its own. It would love you, too, if you were like them, but they hate you because they can't stomach what you stand for. They can't stand that you take a literal view of the Bible, or that you disagree with their immorality. You will be labeled. You will be ostracized. Or, as we've seen in recent years, you will be sued, brought into court, and made to defend yourself.

You might wonder what this has to do with unity. It has everything to do with it. God chose you out of the world to be different. "You are the light of the world. A city that is set on a hill cannot be hidden" (Matthew 5:14). What a powerful reminder! Light is a symbol of purity and truth as opposed to error or ignorance. Ancient towns were often known as sources of light. Many of their buildings were constructed with white limestone that gleamed in the sunshine, and after dark, their windows glowed from within. In daylight or blackest night, you couldn't miss their light. Likewise, God has "called you out of darkness into His marvelous light" (1 Peter 2:9). As a Christ-follower, you are to shine, not blend into the shadows.

You Have a Different Nature

For believers, the call for ecumenical unity should fall on deaf ears for this reason: The Bible strictly forbids it. "Do not be unequally yoked together with unbelievers" (2 Corinthians 6:14).

Yoking is a term that you don't often hear outside of some third-world countries. In biblical times, it was a necessary job. Whenever a field needed plowing, a farmer would go to a carpenter to have his pair of oxen sized up. The carpenter would take measurements of the team and carve a tailor-made wooden yoke that joined them. A good yoke would fit perfectly and ensure the oxen could walk comfortably alongside one another as they worked. A yoke that was fitted properly enabled the farmer to get the job done right.

Today, Jesus says, "Take My yoke upon you" (Matthew 11:29). When we have Christ's yoke upon us, it is easier to walk alongside and work with other believers in advancing His kingdom. The opposite is true when you try to join people who are of two different natures. You can't expect it to work.

I remember reading about a pastor who couldn't believe his eyes as he watched two mismatched animals attempt to plow a field. A Middle Eastern farmer had yoked a donkey to a camel. The camel plodded along on those long legs like he was on vacation, while the donkey scrambled to keep up. At times the donkey would stumble, which made the farmer mad, and he beat the poor beast. It was a horrible sight. Donkeys aren't meant to plow with camels. Oxen with oxen, donkeys with donkeys, even horses and mules yoked with their own kind will work. But mismatches invite disaster. What is obvious in the animal kingdom translates perfectly to the spiritual realm.

To cement his argument against being unequally yoked, Paul asks a series of rhetorical questions that arrive at the same firm conclusion. Let's look at them:

> What fellowship has righteousness with lawlessness? And what communion has light with darkness? And what accord has Christ with Belial? Or what part has a believer with an unbeliever? And what agreement has the temple of God with idols? For you are the temple of the living God (2 Corinthians 6:14-16).

Can righteousness and lawlessness or light and darkness have fellowship and communion together? If we were in a class on logical reasoning, we would determine that these are opposing forces, much like the flesh and the spirit are at odds with each other. Spiritually, one is earthly and perishing. The other is heavenly and eternal. Joining yourself to unbelievers is dangerous and will dilute your devotion to Christ. So, the answer to Paul's question is no.

Note that Paul asks, "What accord has Christ with Belial? Or what part has a believer with an unbeliever?" The word "accord" translates to the Greek word for symphony. Think about it: Paul associates an unbeliever with Belial or Satan. What kind of symphony could Christ possibly have with Satan? The answer is none. The devil's music sounds more like a cacophony than the harmonious beauty of a symphony.

Paul's final question is, "What agreement has the temple of God with idols?" To agree in this sense is to be on the same team or in the same company. I want to stress that the command to not be unequally yoked has nothing to do with activities where we are called to be light. Some situations require Christians to interact with nonbelievers. For instance, do you work for an unbelieving boss, or are you an employer with unbelieving employees? You are working at the same address for a common cause, and in that sense, you and the unbelieving party are yoked to the company's vision. How about sports teams? I think it's awesome to see Christians playing alongside non-Christians and exercising the talents God gave them.

While there are situations where yoking with unbelievers is necessary or permits you to be a good testimony, there are other instances—dating and marriage, worship, and issues of faith—where yoking must be avoided. The Bible says no to relationships with unbelievers when it involves partnering on a spiritual level.

It is impossible to have true fellowship, communion, accord, partnership, or agreement between believers and unbelievers. Why? Because those who have two separate natures, goals, passions, visions, and destinations will always conflict with one another. I also believe that you should do everything possible to steer clear of business partnerships and investments with nonbelievers for those same reasons.

Paul concludes with a theologically powerful statement in verse 16: "You are the temple of the living God." Next to that verse, you should put a little asterisk and write *the local church*. When a church compromises, it becomes a defiled temple. It is in grave danger. But don't think this applies only to the congregation where you worship. Look carefully at what Paul says: "You are the temple." Grand cathedrals and beautiful churches are awe-inspiring, but God does not dwell in buildings made with human hands. A building, nice as it may be, is only a building. *You* are the temple of the living God. This fact alone should help you understand the fallacy of attempting to unite with those who are not connected to the true and living God.

> True unity arises from agreement over truth.

If your neighbor or co-worker invites you to participate in an interfaith prayer meeting, you might be tempted to think, *What's the harm? It doesn't matter if they're praying to different gods. I will pray to mine.* The Bible says don't you dare be unequally yoked! If you want to play some game with them, then by all means, go and have fun. But don't engage in spiritual activity. Ephesians 2:1-2 explains why: "You He made alive, who were dead in trespasses and sins, in which you once walked according to the course of this world, according to the prince of the power of the air, the spirit who now works in the sons of disobedience."

Can you see the division—those who are alive versus those who are dead? The Bible doesn't define non-Christians as merely being diseased; they're dead! Is it physically possible for dead people to have fellowship with those who are alive and well? Of course not, and neither can you do that spiritually.

There is also a clear dividing line between the sons of God and the sons of disobedience. Children of God gravitate toward the truth because they are indwelt by the Holy Spirit. Conversely, children of Satan do not because they are swayed by the spirit of error. Where is unity possible? It's not.

If you think Jesus was neutral on this topic, listen to what He said to a group of religious people: "If God were your Father, you would love Me, for I proceeded forth and came from God; nor have I come of Myself, but He sent Me. Why do you not understand My speech? Because you are not able to listen to My word. You are of your father the devil" (John 8:42-44). I am sure many in the group were fuming, *How outrageous! What an insult!* Yet were not these men of a different religious mindset? Jesus made it clear unity didn't exist between Him and them.

TWO IDENTITIES, ONE CONCLUSION

You may be feeling resistance to some of what you have read up to this point. It is understandable that you may be uncomfortable for any number of reasons, but for those born of God, true unity arises from agreement over truth. To make all this as straightforward as possible, I have compared the identities of believers versus unbelievers. As you go through the lists below, I want you to reach your own conclusion by answering the question, At what point is there a source of unity between believers and unbelievers?

BELIEVERS	UNBELIEVERS
Are of the brethren	Are of the world
Are of God	Are of the devil
Confess Jesus is Lord	Do not confess Jesus is Lord
Are born again	Are children of Satan
Are sons and daughters of God	Are sons and daughters of disobedience

BELIEVERS	UNBELIEVERS
Rally around the Bible	Hold to strange and baffling doctrines
Christ lives in them and through them	Do not have Christ in them
Are indwelt by the Spirit of Truth	Are possessed by the spirit of error
Are hated by the world	Are loved by the world
Believe and stand for the truth	Hate what you believe and stand for
Walk in the light	Walk in darkness
Are righteous	Are lawless
Are the temple of the living God	Are idol worshippers
Are spiritually alive	Are dead in their trespasses and sins

The church needs to stop trying to mix with the things of this world. Try as it might, the church's attempts at ecumenical unity produce nothing more than murky compromise. Imagine putting oil and water into a blender and hitting the mix button. The two appear to merge, but once the blender stops, everything separates. The ingredients resume their natural state, and it's clear they don't mix.

In Revelation 2:20, while addressing the church at Thyatira, Jesus gave a strong rebuke to those who were compromising truth: "Nevertheless I have a few things against you, because you allow that woman Jezebel, who calls herself a prophetess, to teach and seduce My servants to commit sexual immorality and eat things sacrificed to idols." Compromise corrupted the church, but there was still a remnant who had remained faithful to Christ. To them, Jesus said, "Hold fast what you have till I come" (verse 25).

Paul encouraged Timothy in a similar manner when he said, "Hold fast the pattern of sound words which you have heard from me, in faith and love which are in Christ Jesus. That good thing which was committed to you, keep by the Holy Spirit who dwells in us" (2 Timothy 1:13-14). The exhortation to hold fast is a clarion call to tenaciously cling to healthy, life-giving words of truth without compromise.

> Agape is God's unique, sacrificial, self-giving love for mankind— the same love we are to show one another.

Timothy faced false teachers within the church and persecution from outside, while at the same time, Paul was locked in a prison filled with sewage and rats. Compromise would have made their lives easier, and they probably faced the temptation to give in, but both men held fast.

MAKING TRUE CHRISTIAN UNITY A REALITY

I want to bring the topic of unity full circle back to where we began— unity with the brethren. Here is God's design for promoting and protecting unity within the body of Christ:

> Walk worthy of the calling with which you were called, with all lowliness and gentleness, with longsuffering, bearing with one another in love, endeavoring to keep the unity of the Spirit in the bond of peace. There is one body and one Spirit, just as you were called in one hope of your calling; one Lord, one faith, one baptism; one God and Father of all, who is above all, and through all, and in you all (Ephesians 4:1-6).

In this passage, the centerpiece of unity is the three persons of the Trinity—one Father, one Lord, and one Spirit. Theirs is an exclusive oneness that the world does not and cannot participate in, but we can. What an honor and privilege this is!

God called you and me by name to salvation and the union of one body, His body. Now, it is our responsibility to express the reality of that union in lowliness, gentleness, long-suffering toward one another, and bearing with one another in love. Exercising those Christlike attitudes means we will do things like being considerate, refusing to avenge wrongs, and putting up with the idiosyncrasies of others.

But Christian unity goes even further. Ephesians 4:16 says that we are to work together with one another: "The whole body, joined and knit together by what every joint supplies, according to the effective working by which every part does its share, causes growth of the body for the edifying of itself in love."

When believers, regardless of their ethnicity or walk of life, work together under Christ's lordship, everyone benefits. But unity doesn't start and stop with merely laboring together. In addition to the practical working out of our faith, the quality that sets Christian unity apart is agape love. Agape is God's unique, sacrificial, self-giving love for mankind—the same love we are to show one another. Jesus said, "By this all will know that you are My disciples, if you have love for one another" (John 13:35). This is the unity that glorifies God—the kind that we, the brethren, must seek.

The pagan world professes many gods and many lords, but the believer's allegiance belongs to only One. Ephesians 4:5 makes it clear that as believers, we share "one faith," but make no mistake: Faith must be personal before it can become practical. Can you say today that you are wholly committed to a faith that rests solely and wholly upon the biblical truths regarding the risen Lord, Jesus Christ? I pray it is so, for Christ alone is the cornerstone of true Christian unity.

CHAPTER 8

DAZED BY THE DECEPTION
OF NEW TOLERANCE

Today's culture believes tolerance trumps truth. In another era, you would probably say, "It's not possible," because those two virtues go hand in hand. Sadly, that is no longer how people think. Like many other common English words, *tolerant* and *tolerance* have become victims of redefinition in the hands of revisionists. The new tolerance has become a weapon in the war against the truth.

Tolerance is a wonderful virtue, but as a word, it's no longer used in the same way as it was 40 or 50 years ago. I say that because whenever I want to understand the true meaning of a word, I turn to my 1828 version of Webster's dictionary. In 1806, Noah Webster initially published *A Compendious Dictionary of the English Language*, the first truly American dictionary. But immediately following its publication, Webster went to work on another. In 1828, the *American Dictionary of the English Language* was published. Webster learned 26 languages other than English to help him in his research of the origins and meanings of English words. I think Webster's definitions of *tolerance* and *tolerate* far surpass those we are being force-fed today:

> *Tolerance:* The power or capacity of enduring; or the act of enduring.

> *Tolerate:* To suffer to be or to be done without prohibition or hinderance; to allow or permit negatively, by not preventing; not to restrain; as, to *tolerate* opinions or practices.

> "The law of love *tolerates* no vice, and patronizes every virtue." G. Spring

These definitions tell us that we are to suffer or endure someone else's belief even if we disagree with them. I also want to point out Webster's revealing side note following the definition of *tolerance*. It reads, "Little used. But intolerance is in common use." Is that not indicative of our world? When people tell us, "You must be tolerant," we must ask ourselves, *What are they saying, and why are they saying it?* This reminds me of the scene in the movie *The Wizard of Oz*, where Dorothy looks around, then says, "We're not in Kansas anymore." The contemporary usage of *intolerant* in favor of the classical definition of *tolerant* has left many feeling like Dorothy and wondering, *What has happened?*

Tolerance is a virtue we extend toward someone with whom we don't agree. We allow their view to be presented. We don't whine, protest, picket, and refuse their right to give an opposing viewpoint. You see, there are times when we will disagree with others, and it is incumbent upon us, as fellow humans, to extend tolerance to one another. For example, I am a bit hyper and naturally go back and forth between various tasks and activities over the course of a day. Now, to someone who is mellow and orderly, that might be irritating. But it's okay. I don't expect them to adopt or even agree with my methodology, but as a mark of civility and tolerance, I hope that they will endure it.

Stripping the word *tolerance* of its original meaning has opened it to reinterpretation by anyone and everyone as they see fit. It is a lot like someone walking into the Mercedes Benz factory in Stuttgart, Germany, and saying, "I'll take one of those fenders, this type of headlight, and that roof. I really like the taillights you used a decade ago, and, oh, I don't want the chassis you picked out, so let's substitute this one. I know the car will look strange when you are finished, but that suits me just fine." The Mercedes engineers would throw you out because they are dedicated to building according to a car's precise specifications. Without attention to detail, they're going to end up with a chaotic mess—precisely what has happened to the meaning of *tolerance*.

Christians need to exercise great wisdom when dealing with the world's intolerant behavior masquerading as a virtue. Otherwise, this dangerous deception will neutralize and destroy the body of Jesus Christ.

THE NEW TOLERANCE DECIDES WHAT IS TOLERATED

In America, some have confused our First Amendment rights with intolerance, turning them into volatile political and social issues. Yes, the redefinition of *tolerance* has exerted its influence in those areas, but of equal concern are the politicians themselves, who are attempting to take this revised meaning from the secular into the sacred. We have watched in disbelief as leaders in Washington, DC, have tried to ban evangelism because they felt it fueled and stoked religious passions. Of course it does, but is religious passion wrong? Yet today, if a Christian says to someone, "I disagree with your belief," it can be labeled a hate crime. It makes no sense that simply verbalizing "Jesus loves you and wants you to go to heaven" can qualify as hate speech.

The end result of the newly defined tolerance is that it weakens and dilutes the church's strength, morphs it into society, and removes its uniqueness in the world.

The strength of the church is the power of the gospel. When a Christian missionary goes out into the mission field, do you know what they do? They get a job. They work alongside the natives of that country as

steelworkers, longshoremen, teachers, shopkeepers, etc. The missionar-
ies make friends and love them as Christ would have them to do, which
naturally builds bridges for sharing the gospel. Inevitably, lives are radically changed and souls are saved. This sounds reasonable to you and
me, yet the secular world doesn't see it that way. But I believe their view
is intellectually dishonest and hypocritical.

Our culture demands tolerance, but the minute it's discovered that you
are a Christian, that same culture suddenly becomes intolerant. Believers are told, "Your opinions are hurtful and hateful, and you need to
keep them to yourself." If you share the good news of the gospel because
you care about someone and want them to experience forgiveness of sin,
you're told, "You are doing them harm." Would it be better to pat them
on the back and let them go straight to hell? The answer is no, but that's
what the devil wants.

I, like many others, wonder how we have reached this point. Have
we become so immature that I, as a Christ-follower, can't talk to a Mus-
lim friend about religion, and vice versa? Does the knowledge that we
have significant differences mean we can't go out for tacos together and
talk things through? How have we become so shallow?

If a person wants to believe a certain way and practice that belief
within the bounds of our laws, they have the freedom to do so. I will
respect their decision, and so should you. Will I agree with them? No. I
don't have to agree with them just as they don't have to agree with me.
We can amicably agree to disagree—this is true tolerance. Unfortunately,
according to the new definition of tolerance, it doesn't work that way.

In today's culture, individuals are entitled to express their views, and
everyone else must respect those views—that is, until you want to talk
about Jesus Christ. Mention Jesus, and you are suddenly branded as
intolerant because you say, "Jesus is the way, the truth, and the life" (see
John 14:6). What about bowing your head and praying in Jesus' name?
That too is offensive and divisive and must stop.

Several years ago, at a local National Day of Prayer gathering, our mayor stood on the lawn of city hall and read a widely circulated poem entitled "The New School Prayer." Its origins are undocumented, but it is credited to an anonymous student. I think it bears repeating because kids are often more willing to speak up when adults won't or don't.

Now I sit me down in school
Where praying is against the rule
For this great nation under God
Finds mention of Him very odd.
If Scripture now the class recites,
It violates the Bill of Rights.
And anytime my head I bow
Becomes a federal matter now.
Our hair can be purple, orange, or green,
That's no offense; it's a freedom scene.
The law is specific, the law is precise.
Prayers spoken aloud are a serious vice.
For praying in a public hall
Might offend someone with no faith at all.
In silence alone we must meditate,
God's name is prohibited by the state.
We're allowed to cuss and dress like freaks,
And pierce our noses, tongues, and cheeks.
They've outlawed guns, but FIRST the Bible.
To quote the Good Book makes me liable.
We can elect a pregnant Senior Queen,
And the unwed daddy, our Senior King.
It's "inappropriate" to teach right from wrong,
We're taught that such "judgments" do not belong.
We can get our condoms and birth controls,
Study witchcraft, vampires, and totem poles.
But the Ten Commandments are not allowed,
No Word of God must reach this crowd.
It's scary here I must confess,

When chaos reigns the school's a mess.
So, Lord, this silent plea I make:
Should I be shot; my soul please take!
Amen

Following her reading, the mayor made this comment: "It's not easy to be in the position of mayor, and to say these things, but I'm going to keep on saying them." Oh, that God would raise up a spiritual army with her courage!

THE NEW TOLERANCE DISMISSES ABSOLUTES

I have heard it said that people will do anything when they believe God is dead. Our culture's condition proves the validity of that statement. Right and wrong are now subjective and open for interpretation. Sins like anger, violence, fornication, adultery, lying, drunkenness, and thievery are now widely tolerated and justified. But if the perpetrators are caught or exposed, their reasoning tends to run along one of these lines:

- You must accept me unconditionally—this is just who I am.
- I can't help myself. My behavior isn't my fault—you see, I have a disease.
- I enjoy what I'm doing and don't see any harm in it.
- I don't need to comply with your rules because I didn't make them, and I don't acknowledge the God who you say did make those rules.

If you accept those kinds of excuses, it stands to reason that you can't criticize or punish a tagger caught spray-painting your fence or building multiple times. Tagging could be rationalized as an expression of free speech, even though it's vandalizing private property.

Or how about disturbing the peace? I live near a greenbelt with a little stream, trees everywhere, and a walking path. At the entrance is a sign that reads: By the City of Chino Hills ordinance, no profanity allowed. The wording is straightforward and meant to keep that place enjoyable for everyone. Yet I've witnessed teens walking by, pointing to the sign, and intentionally blurting out profanities. I want to say, "Wait, can't you read?" Sometimes I have my doubts. In this age of redefined tolerance, swearing up a storm is chalked up to being literacy challenged, or in the case of the teens, they're just kids. Never mind that they are ruining everyone else's experience.

You might believe that unrestrained tagging and disturbing the peace are petty and deserving of tolerance, but these kinds of behaviors set the stage for future firestorms. When a society condones youthful misbehavior and something bigger comes along, there is no ground of truth to stand on. This is why when a kid is shot dead by another kid wanting to be somebody important in a gang, you hear a neighbor say, "We can't hold the children responsible. They don't know what they're doing." The shooter would also argue, "My father wasn't around when I was growing up. My mother abused and neglected me. I have nobody. I've got to look out for number one, and fitting in with a gang family makes sense." But the Bible says that the kind of logic used by the neighbor and the shooter is deceptively twisted: "Woe to those who call evil good, and good evil" (Isaiah 5:20).

We live in a society bent on having its way, but that works only when people lower their expectations and values. In America, we reinforce lower standards through laws that make light of and sometimes seem to flaunt sinful behavior. But it wasn't always this way, and the US Supreme Court building proves it. Carved into the marble frieze directly above the Supreme Court's chief justice's chair is Israel's lawgiver, Moses. Seated with a tablet in each arm featuring Roman numerals I through X, Moses is twice as big as the other lawgivers depicted. The Ten Commandments were also carved into the courtroom doors, on the support frame of the courtroom's bronze gates, and in the library woodwork.

The Supreme Court is only one of many places in our nation where

God and the Bible are exalted. The countless carvings, statues, pictures, monuments, and documents are more than symbols; they are our history. Yet, in the name of tolerance, Christians are forced to accept laws and court rulings that violate the absolutes of Holy Scripture. The United States was long viewed as a Christian nation, but in recent decades, as governing bodies have continued to validate godlessness, Christianity has become viewed as an aberrant belief system to be squashed.

THE NEW TOLERANCE SETS THE BOUNDARIES

"Stay within our prescribed boundaries" is fast becoming the secularist's mantra. In my home state of California, two churches—one in Sun Valley, the other in San Jose—would not close their doors because of COVID restrictions and were sued by the state. Both cases went to court, and both pastors and their congregations were fully vindicated, ultimately triumphing over the state's intolerance of religious freedom. But it is a sad commentary that there weren't more willing to stand and exercise their right to remain open and not forsake assembling together (see Hebrews 10:25).

The demand for the new kind of tolerance is driven in part by political correctness, which I believe has seeped into, and in many cases, infiltrated, the church. As an example, I point to user-friendly pulpit messages that don't shake, rattle, or convict anybody. Pastors refrain from saying certain words in their sermons and on social media for fear of reprisal. During the 2022 election cycle, I took a stand against a proposed amendment to California's state constitution that allowed unrestricted abortion from conception through delivery. When censors heard me mention the proposition from the pulpit and post about it on social media, I was consigned to Instagram jail. I wish I could say that biblical values prevailed at the ballot box, but fear and apathy won the day.

Since then, I've been shadow banned and temporarily removed from Facebook, and I am not alone. Others, whom I will not name, have been deplatformed and scandalized because they could not be silenced.

Whether we are forced to close down or pressured to stay silent, we should ask ourselves: Is this what freedom and tolerance look like?

American believers have never experienced religious persecution en masse, but if we continue down this road, one day, we will find ourselves silenced entirely or worse. I know it seems inconceivable in a country founded upon freedom of speech and religion. Still, if global history proves anything, it is this: The persecution and arrest of pastors and church leaders will follow and increase.

The church needs to wake up and stand up! The alternative is to join the ranks of believers in totalitarian nations that claim the right to control the whole person, including their beliefs. That is a sobering thought, but one with biblical precedent.

In Acts 5:28-29, we read about the disciples preaching Jesus Christ everywhere. Along came the religious hierarchy, who said, "Did we not strictly command you not to teach in this name? And look, you have filled Jerusalem with your doctrine, and intend to bring this Man's blood on us!" But Peter and the other apostles answered and said, "We ought to obey God rather than men."

Peter's statement came straight from the Holy Spirit and informed us of how we are to respond when a nation goes awry and is estranged from God. Yes, we are to obey the laws of the land, as Romans chapter 13 commands—until those laws directly violate the Word of God.

THE NEW TOLERANCE ISN'T LOVING

Some Christians hold to the idea that we need to argue with those who disagree with us, or spiritually wrestle them to the ground in the hopes that they will come around to our way of thinking. Tolerance doesn't work that way. Instead of fighting against them, we should care for them because we are concerned for their soul.

The Bible says, "Faithful are the wounds of a friend, but the kisses of an enemy are deceitful" (Proverbs 27:6). With that in mind, what would you do if the following were to happen? You see your neighbor back his car out of his driveway and leave. Then you notice the guy next door go over to that neighbor's house and stay for a couple of hours. In the days that follow, this guy next door continues to make these visits. One afternoon, you have a chance to talk with the guy, and ask him, "Hey, what's going on?" He answers, "Oh, Mrs. So-and-So and me are having a little fling." What do you say? Keep in mind what Proverbs says about the difference between a friend and an enemy. And remember that the enemy of our souls is the ultimate deceiver.

The loving thing to do would be to say, "You don't want to do that. God says that the person who commits adultery will not go to heaven. Think about what you are doing. At the very least, her husband could really mess you up—even shoot you. I love you enough to tell you the truth." An enemy would think, *It's really none of my business. He's just having a little fun. I've got to be tolerant.* But can you see how harmful that deceitful way of thinking is? The same person who says, "If it feels right, go ahead and do what you want" would never allow the neighbor to abuse their pet out of hatred. When the shoe is on the other foot, they fold because their foundation is faulty.

Faced with unrelenting pressure to accept all lifestyles, many churches are surrendering their moral ground despite a clear biblical mandate to do otherwise. This leaves Christ-followers who stand on biblical truth stigmatized as unloving and intolerant. Yet God's Word is unambiguous about sinful behavior. For example, read what Romans 1 clearly says about same-sex relationships:

> For this reason God gave them up to vile passions. For even their women exchanged the natural use for what is against nature. Likewise also the men, leaving the natural use of the woman, burned in their lust for one another, men with men committing what is shameful, and receiving in themselves the penalty of their error which was due (Romans 1:26-27).

Do you think God says to Himself, "I don't know if I should

have said that because things are getting a little dicey in this area today"? No. God, in whom there is "no variation or shadow of turning" (James 1:17), hasn't changed His mind.

> The next time you go out your front door and into the world, be tolerant as God is—loving, forgiving, gracious, and merciful to the outcast while intolerant of evil, wrongdoing, and godlessness.

None of what I have said regarding sexuality is hateful or intolerant; it's quite the opposite. It is loving and kind because I am looking beyond the here and now with people's ultimate good in mind—the hope they will become saved.

Reach out to the homosexual, lesbian, and sexually confused person and show them the love of Jesus. Ask them, "Do you want real love? Let me tell you about real love," and then read 1 Corinthians 6:9-11 and John 15:13 to them.

> Do you not know that the unrighteous will not inherit the kingdom of God? Do not be deceived. Neither fornicators, nor idolaters, nor adulterers, nor homosexuals, nor sodomites, nor thieves, nor covetous, nor drunkards, nor revilers, nor extortioners will inherit the kingdom of God. And such were some of you. But you were washed, but you were sanctified, but you were justified in the name of the Lord Jesus and by the Spirit of our God.

> Greater love has no one than this, than to lay down one's life for his friends.

Then say to them, "Jesus laid down His life for you, my friend."

I deliberately chose those verses because you've heard the claim that God is intolerant. Maybe you have wondered if that is true. I urge you to take a moment to think back on your life. Maybe your sins weren't sexual in nature, but you drank to excess, coveted other people's possessions, or did other things prohibited in the Bible. Proverbs 29:1 says, "He who is often rebuked, and hardens his neck, will suddenly be destroyed, and that without remedy," yet here you are. Before you became a Christian, God waited with patience and mercy and did not end your life. You weren't in a fatal accident. You didn't have a stroke or heart attack. Did God take you or me away in our rebellion? No, He waited. God endured our foolishness and rebellion. True to Noah Webster's definition, God was tolerant. "Don't you see how wonderfully kind, tolerant, and patient God is with you? "Does this mean nothing to you? Can't you see that his kindness is intended to turn you from your sin?" (Romans 2:4 NLT).

The next time you go out your front door and into the world, be tolerant as God is—loving, forgiving, gracious, and merciful to the outcast while intolerant of evil, wrongdoing, and godlessness. Remember to distinguish between sin itself and the lost and lonely sinner who needs the love of God. And be willing to bear with their intolerance so that you might guide them to the love found only in Jesus Christ.

TRUE TOLERANCE SHOWS OTHERS A BETTER WAY

People often condemn the Bible because certain scriptures don't seem inclusive, and in a sense, they are right. Not only are they not inclusive, but they are also very exclusive. Much of the New Testament is directed to individuals who share a unique supernatural closeness. I have worshipped in biblically sound churches in distant cities and foreign lands and felt right at home, even when we didn't speak the same language. How is it possible? *Koinonia*—the Greek word that describes the fellowship, sharing, and communion believers have with one another.

Koinonia fellowship is exclusive to brothers and sisters in Christ. But does this type of unique fellowship qualify as intolerant and mean-spirited? Does it automatically mean that we will destroy abortion clinics in our fight against abortion? No! We urge moms to choose life and pray for every person within those clinics' walls to come to Christ. Does our oneness mean that we persecute and attack Muslims or Hindus because we worship the God of the Bible? On the contrary, if they were choking, we should resuscitate them. Or if they were injured, we should donate blood to save their lives. Can we expect them to reciprocate if needed? We shouldn't. Christians live by a higher standard that does not allow us to turn our backs on someone in need, even our enemies.

> Our enemies should be among the most blessed people on the face of the earth.

Our enemies should be among the most blessed people on the face of the earth. Here is what Scripture urges us to do for them: "If your enemy is hungry, feed him; if he is thirsty, give him a drink; for in so doing you will heap coals of fire on his head. Do not be overcome by evil, but overcome evil with good" (Romans 12:20-21).

One of the best examples I've seen of tolerance toward an enemy was when my wife and I attended Calvary Chapel Costa Mesa. We were in the bookstore, and out near the street was a radical group getting ready to storm the church. Standing on the curb between the parking lot and the group was one of the pastors. Years prior, he had played football and was still a very big and muscular man, which made what happened next even more amazing. A tiny man from the crowd stepped in front of him and began poking his finger at his chest. The pastor's neck veins were bulging, but he stood still without retaliating.

Afterward, when asked, "Didn't you want to hurt that guy?" he said, "I did in the beginning. But then I realized how pitiful this man was, and I began to pray for him." That, my friend, is the Spirit of God at work, diffusing a tense and ugly situation.

Our enemies in the workplace, on the home front, or around town should be able to say, "See that guy or gal? They're the best enemy I've ever had. My life is blessed because of them. I'm going to keep them as my enemy."

Our culture has moved to the far side of hypersensitivity, which, in turn, has led to a major movement within Christian circles to make the church seem tolerant as the world defines it. Personally, I don't see anywhere in the Bible a calling for us to do that. Whenever believers allow themselves to be guided by the feelings of unbelievers, they're right where Satan wants them: fearful of speaking the truth.

Believer, tolerance, in its truest sense, is not for the faint of heart. The Lord knows that you and I live in a world filled with hostility and anger. It would be great if, as soon as we were born again, we went straight to heaven. But by the decree of God, we remain in this world. If that weren't true, there would be no one on Earth who could show the lost that there is a better way.

The apostle Paul wrote a reminder to the Corinthian church that can help guide our mindset when it comes to tolerance as the world sees it. He said, "I wrote to you in my epistle not to keep company with sexually immoral people. Yet I certainly did not mean with the sexually immoral people of this world, or with the covetous, or extortioners, or idolaters, since then you would need to go out of the world" (1 Corinthians 5:9-10). We are not to keep company with those who name the name of Christ but habitually practice sin. Yet Paul isn't talking about believers here—these are unbelievers.

God has asked us to go out into the unbelieving world and be around those who commit such sins. Don't build yourself a Christian fortress and hide there. Go with wisdom and understanding to influence the world for the glory of God. Go to those who are hurting and love them without assimilating their beliefs. This is what it means to be in the world but not of it.

Combatting the rising tide of the new tolerance requires us to be strengthened through the Holy Spirit in our inner man, the place where the Spirit changes and renews our thinking (see Ephesians 3:16). It is there that the Holy Spirit fortifies our resolve to live according to God's will. We grow stronger when we daily realign our thinking with the Bible. Romans 12:1 commands all believers, "Do not be conformed to this world, but be transformed by the renewing of your mind, that you may prove what is that good and acceptable and perfect will of God." Do you want to be strong and wise in response to today's mixed-up world? Renew your mind!

Like physical strength training, growing spiritually strong does not happen overnight. It comes in degrees, and it takes discipline. Your strength builds up every time you intentionally choose to submit to God's revealed will rather than conform to the dictates of society.

But beware—and this is important: Satan will not leave your resolve unchallenged. He will continue to woo you through devilish and persuasive arguments. He'll tug at your heartstrings through family members who are living ungodly lifestyles. When that happens, pray! Ask for the Spirit's empowerment. Because He dwells in you, He makes the vast resources of heaven available for your aid.

Let's face it: We are more than different—we are not of this world. The Bible says that we are earthen vessels—essentially clay pots—but we have the Holy Spirit's power residing within. He freely gives us the ability and inner fortitude to stand firm, making us potential dynamos for the kingdom of God. May He work in and through us for His glory and the salvation of many!

CHAPTER 9

DAZED BY THE DECEPTION OF THE WORLD

B roadway Avenue is one of the oldest streets in New York City, and its claim to fame are the sights and sounds of its productions. Imagine that you are seated in one of those spectacular Broadway shows. The lights dim and the orchestra fills the theater with sound. Onstage, the curtains slide open, and you see famous and want-to-be famous actors begin their performance. Each character has a personality, passion, and pursuit, but they're all part of a single narrative.

Outside the theater, there is a bigger play unfolding before us on the world stage. Right now, a select group of progressive thinkers—elite men and women of position and power—are maneuvering to change life as we know it, but not for the good. They are what we call *bad actors*. The term *bad actor* is an idiom for a person or organization that is harmful, illegal, morally wrong, or deceptive.

The bad actors among global elites believe the world is ready for change. They say that for too long, the world has been under the sway of the West—predominantly, the United States. In fact, to those who promote progressive ideologies, America *is* the problem. Why does this matter? One of the tactics of deception is to vilify what is good to advance what is evil. America is viewed by many as still operating under predominantly Christian values. These values are what have made us a viable, free, and liberated society—yet progressives view these values as a hindrance to the advancement of their ideologies.

The circumstances of our day demand that none of us take things at face value, and as we've already seen, it's incumbent that we question everything. Please do not blindly accept what you are reading in these pages because it seems plausible. And I am certainly not asking you to believe something because I say it is true. Rather, I am asking you to make every effort to educate yourself and ask the Holy Spirit to guide you into all truth (see John 16:13)—it is His pleasure to do so.

Some of the issues I will cover in this chapter have to do with matters many do not see eye to eye on. Regardless of where you might stand on these issues, my point in bringing them up is to demonstrate a bigger problem taking place behind the scenes: a global agenda that seeks to increase government control and deprive people of their freedoms.

Regarding global bad actors and their institutions, it is vital that we understand how what appear to be stand-alone events are connected to gaining control by whatever means possible—namely, by manipulating facts to create a crisis and then jumping in to provide the solution. We have looked at some of these points in previous chapters, but now I want to show how they intersect.

DECEIVED BY THOSE WHO MANAGE INFORMATION
...by Silencing Voices

Information is power. Historically, great enemies of freedom have often succeeded in overtaking their enemies by controlling the narrative. Currently, entities with vast resources have embarked on a large-scale mission to sequester books that they deem unacceptable.[1] They aim to remove from the marketplace books and authors that threaten their worldview. They do this to silence opposing or controversial ideas. Authors write to be published, but if publishers are afraid that booksellers won't buy an author's material, the manuscript is rejected or shelved.[2] Recently we have witnessed the rise of censorship through sensitivity readers who flag offensive content, stereotypes, bias, etc. for authors and publishers. It isn't only political works that this form of censorship affects; these vigilantes have gone after popular literature such as Ian Fleming's James Bond novels and childhood classics like Roald Dahl's *James and the Giant Peach* and *Willy Wonka and the Chocolate Factory*.[3] Sometimes authors purposefully use provocative language or dark humor, but in today's cancel culture, that must be avoided—such content must be edited lest it offends liberal sensitivities.

...by Erasing History

A historian friend of mine told me that historical books are also being targeted for removal from the public square. If there is anything we can learn from history, it is that whenever those in power have sought control, they have done so by demoralizing and intimidating those whom they consider enemies. To do this, they first eliminate—or, at the very least, dilute—history itself. By tampering with the record of past civilizations and peoples, they remove the capacity to compare the past with the present day. This hinders people's ability to know the pitfalls they should avoid. In other words, the old saying is true: Those who do not know history are doomed to repeat it.

Eliminating or refusing to publish true accounts of the past erases knowledge. As strange as it may sound, this plays a tremendous role in making deception possible. That is what happens in George Orwell's science fiction novel *1984*, in which history is constantly being rewritten, and only a select few know the actual truth.

Once you control what is known about history, it is easier to control the masses. You can fabricate new thoughts and ideas, such as this one spreading through academia today: the holocaust against the Jews in Germany and Eastern Europe never happened. It's a myth.

> The last bastion of truth is and will be the remnant of God's people who remain curious and dedicated truth seekers.

When erasing history altogether isn't possible, reinventing it suits progressives just fine. If those in power remove truthful information from the halls of education and elsewhere so that people cannot examine it, then the seeds of doubt can be sown, and eventually germinate and bear fruit.

Jonathan Swift summed up the truth regarding lies and misinformation in a 1710 article in the English political newspaper *The Examiner*. The quote has seen a lot of mileage, variously attributed to Charles Spurgeon, Mark Twain, and Winston Churchill, among others. Swift's writing is in old English, so read it slowly. His observation is timeless:

> Besides, as the vilest Writer has his Readers, so the greatest Liar has his Believers; and it often happens, that if a Lie be believ'd only for an Hour, it has done its Work, and there is no farther occasion for it. Falsehood flies, and the Truth comes limping after it; so that when Men come to be undeceiv'd, it is too late; the jest is over, and the Tale has had its Effect.[4]

The enemy has succeeded when the tale has had its effect, and deception has taken hold in a person's life.

As a pastor, it is my job to educate people. I am supposed to teach them to depend on God. My calling is to encourage and excite others to be students, first and foremost, of the Bible. And to get them to explore the amazing world around them. I firmly believe that the last bastion of truth is and will be the remnant of God's people who remain curious and dedicated truth seekers.

DECEIVED BY THOSE WHO CREATE CRISES
...by Obscuring Medical Data

The article's title, "Increased Heart Failure Deaths Linked to Extreme Hot and Cold," caught my eye. It had been a cold winter, so I was intrigued. The article purported to show there has been a noticeable increase in heart failure in deaths that are linked to extreme heat and cold.

The article focused on a study coauthored by experts from Harvard's T.H. Chan School of Public Health. It looked at more than 32 million cardiovascular deaths over four decades from more than two dozen countries. Now I was really interested. The number of case studies was significant, and if weather plays such a significant role in my heart health, I should be concerned about how global warming affects my health. Right? Wrong. The study found that for every 1,000 cardiovascular deaths, only 2.2 additional deaths could be attributed to *extreme* hot days, and only 9.1 additional deaths to *extreme* cold days.

The headline was sensational, but the research failed to deliver substance. Nowhere did the article define what was meant by the term *extreme*, or even what temperatures were considered optimal. Nor was there mention of how and why a person would be exposed to such temperatures. The article connected a small number of deaths to extreme weather patterns that, if you believe media hype, will soon be upon us. Never mind that those patterns have yet to materialize. The whole point was to generate worry about what might happen. At least, that was the impression the study's coauthor, Barrak Alahmad, gave: "The current challenge now is the environment and what climate change might hold for us."[5]

I want to mention the COVID pandemic here as well because, at the time of this writing, we continue to learn of the previously inconceivable deception fostered by erroneous data. In the opening days of the pandemic, we were told the situation was dire and would remain so into the foreseeable future without quick mass vaccination. Adding to the confusion, the scientific community failed to provide clear data on how many people died of COVID alone versus in conjunction with other illnesses.

Cable News Network (CNN) medical analyst and *Washington Post* columnist Dr. Leana Wen admitted in 2023 that the medical community has, and still is, overcounting the number of COVID deaths and hospitalizations. Wen cited various sources claiming that most patients diagnosed with COVID were admitted to hospitals for some other illness. She referenced infectious-disease physician Shira Doron, who figured out that "in recent months, only about 30 percent of total hospitalizations with COVID were primarily attributed to the virus" in Massachusetts hospitals, for example. Wen also recounted Doron's experience at Tufts Medical Center. "During some days, the proportion of those hospitalized because of COVID were as low as 10 percent of the total number reported who had COVID."[6]

What's my point? We are witnessing unprecedented deceptions involving our personal health. Experts are manipulating facts and data to obscure the truth. Think about it: If a virus is presented as unstoppable unless you hibernate and vaccinate, won't you willingly agree and fall in line with the authorities? And if you don't? In countries around the world, we saw governments call upon citizens to shun and expose those in noncompliance. That alone should raise red flags. But the deception goes even further.

What if questionable computer-driven weather models can convince you that the weather will turn increasingly deadly and affect your health? Won't you, out of fear, get on board with the international climate accords? For millions, the answer is a resounding yes!

...by Peddling Climate Alarmism

Nearly every environmental agency and news outlet is beating the drum labeled climate change, but there has been a shift as of late. More and more, the issue is being called a major crisis. Change can be perceived as occurring gradually over time, but by using the term *crisis*, activists are able to paint the situation in a whole different light. The effects of changes can be lessened, but crises demand swift and sometimes drastic action. Call it what you will, this is an exaggerated narrative causing needless panic. Despite media claims to the opposite, there is no evidence that a climate crisis looms in our future. Are there fluctuations in weather patterns? Yes. But as the following article points out, it is a common phenomenon.

> Temperatures clearly are rising, but a National Oceanic and Atmospheric Administration reconstruction of global temperatures over the past one million years, using data from ice cores, shows both warming and cooling periods.

From the same article:

> *The New York Times* recently reported that people were cutting Europe's forests for firewood because fossil fuels were too costly or unavailable. This reflects the desperation that unnecessary and shortsighted U.S. and European policies have created.

> Global mean sea level has been increasing at about 3.3 mm per year since satellite measurements began in 1992. Over the course of a century, that works out to about 13 inches, hardly a crisis, and even if it continues, adaptation would be straightforward. Moreover, because recent temperature increases have resulted from both natural and anthropogenic causes, it is difficult to separate out the human-caused component of the sea level increase. Arctic sea ice has been declining, while the Antarctic Sea ice has been stable or growing.[7]

The above quotes are from an article written in 2022, but climate deception is longstanding, as this 2011 quote from *Forbes* shows:

> A new batch of 5,000 emails among scientists central to the assertion that humans are causing a global warming crisis were anonymously released to the public yesterday, igniting

a new firestorm of controversy nearly two years to the day
after similar emails ignited the Climategate scandal.

Three themes are emerging from the newly released emails:
(1) prominent scientists central to the global warming debate
are taking measures to conceal rather than disseminate underlying data and discussions; (2) these scientists view global
warming as a political "cause" rather than a balanced scientific inquiry and (3) many of these scientists frankly admit
to each other that much of the science is weak and depen-
dent on deliberate manipulation of facts and data.[8]

Deception never comes across as deceitful, which is the whole point.
French writer and statesman Andre Malraux said, "Man is not what he
thinks he is. He is what he hides."[9] I want to add that people can seem
well intentioned, but if they are hiding something, you need to ask why.

Climate alarmism is encouraged and propagated by advocates who
cry that it is of the utmost importance to save the planet. Not surpris-
ingly, they will not be affected by their restrictive policies—some even
justify their exclusion.[10] Nonetheless, their agenda harms the people they
claim to care about, especially the poor and disadvantaged.

Often the poorest countries have the most dangerous ecological envi-
ronments. Due to their poverty, they lack the necessary resources to better
people's lives. Deaths and stillbirths remain high, and morbidity continues to rise. This is in stark contrast to Western nations.

Pollution and its harmful by-products are on a consistent downward
trend in most industrialized and technologically advanced countries. The
environment is cleaner, and longevity is on the uptick. Overall, Western
society enjoys a higher standard of living. Yet the climate community
continues to issue edicts that we must erase those advancements. They
say that we must stop eating cattle, driving cars, drilling for oil, or working toward nuclear energy as a power source. These kinds of prohibitions
promise to cascade humanity, rich and poor, back into the Dark Ages.

Why would anyone believe in and promote actions that harm rather than help? The Bible says that ultimately, this is a spiritual issue. Romans 1:25 talks about how people exchange "the truth of God for the lie," and worship and serve the creature rather than the Creator. The worship of the earth has made inroads into some of the most powerful administrations and institutions on the planet, including the United Nations.

The United Nations' Office of the High Commissioner for Human Rights released a news article entitled "Climate Change the Greatest Threat the World Has Ever Faced, UN Expert Warns." According to them, climate change—not international terrorism, totalitarian regimes with nuclear capabilities, collapsing economies, disintegration of the family unit, poverty, nor lack of educational resources—is the number one issue that should keep us up at night. Connecting the dots of mankind's health and well-being to climate change may seem like a stretch of the imagination, but that is precisely what the United Nations has attempted to do.

> Throughout the world, human rights are being negatively impacted and violated as a consequence of climate change. This includes the right to life, health, food, development, self-determination, water and sanitation, work, adequate housing and freedom from violence, sexual exploitation, trafficking, and slavery, said Ian Fry, UN Special Rapporteur on the promotion and protection of human rights in the context of climate change.[11]

Perhaps you, like me, find it incomprehensible that climate change is having an effect on self-determination, human trafficking, and slavery, yet that is the claim of this international body. And because it's the United Nations, people readily accept its assessment without question. But these claims are deceptive manipulation, pure and simple.

DECEIVED BY THOSE WHO PROFESS TO HAVE ANSWERS
Earlier, I used the illustration of a Broadway play to talk about the

world stage. But I had not yet mentioned that frequently, these plays feature a villain as well as a hero who shows up and saves the day in the nick of time. This scenario isn't limited to Broadway productions. It is playing out right in front of us. If there were a global marque, it would announce: Now appearing on the world stage in Davos, Switzerland: Klaus Schwab and the World Economic Forum.

For most of the year, Davos is nothing more than a ski resort in the Swiss Alps. But for one week in January, Davos is *the* destination for global elites. Since 1971, Davos has become synonymous with the annual meeting of the World Economic Forum (WEF). It is where movers and shakers convene to discuss their visionary plans for curing global ills, thus charting a course for the planet's future. Davos is where we first heard founder and executive chairman Klaus Schwab's opportunistic call for a Great Reset. "The pandemic represents a rare but narrow window of opportunity to reflect, reimagine, and reset our world."[12]

The goal of the reset that Schwab advocates is to change the very fabric of civilization and herald a new world order. The WEF is a big promoter of the globalist concept of smart cities and a shared economy. According to this vision, you will own nothing, have no privacy, and be happy.[13]

Looking into the future has been the nexus of Klaus Schwab's statement that the WEF seeks to bring answers to problems as they are discovered. Let the phrase "bring answers to problems" sink in for a moment. Problem-solving ideas sound great, until you realize that those claiming to have answers also have devious plans to implement.

I know this sounds sinister, but there are people and groups with the mindset that it is okay to destabilize a culture to further an agenda. They realize that by creating or accentuating an existing problem and positioning themselves as having the solution, they can put themselves in the driver's seat and claim more power. I believe the WEF is attempting to do that.

The WEF's annual meetings in Davos have become a window into the minds of prominent globalists. It is no secret that the WEF has been the past nursery for leaders such as Barack Obama, Justin Trudeau, Volodymyr Zelensky, and even Vladimir Putin. In 2023, the WEF leadership hosted a record number of global leaders that included heads of state, finance ministers, foreign ministers, trade ministers, governors of central banks, and chief executive officers of some of the world's largest firms, along with what the group refers to as teenage "change-makers."

Two questions come to mind: What is behind what looks like a benign gathering of well-groomed elites in Switzerland? Why are leaders giving credence to a nongovernmental organization whose members suggest some of the most bizarre and disturbing global objectives imaginable? Yet each year, attendees of the WEF return home with a renewed determination to move toward a global state. As an entity, the forum desires to propose and implement policies that affect borders, global economies, business models, and the environment, or what they refer to as the global commons.

Their efforts are paving the way for what they hope to be a future government that will establish, under one umbrella, a global community led by a handful of dominant totalitarian leaders—all the while smiling as they do it. Klaus Schwab put his personal spin on this in a 2016 tweet: "Globalization is not the problem. A lack of leadership is the problem."[14]

Swiss MP Bastien Girod is the type of leader the WEF is looking for with his upbeat vision of a utopia designed for you and me. Part of Girod's pitch for our future includes government control over how a region's populace is organized because electric cars aren't enough to help reduce our carbon footprint. Girod proposes that governments funnel people into restructured cities designed around carbon controls and make individual car ownership illegal. Somehow this will promote happiness because everything you need will be right within your neighborhood. Want to take a spur-of-the-moment drive to someplace outside of your area? You'll need a permit. What this proposal really means is tight living spaces, mass transit, bicycles for all, lower standards of living, and a big power grab.

These ideas make citizens who believe in freedom of movement, and everything that comes along with it, cringe. I am talking about the simple freedom to choose where you work and where your children will attend school, even if it means a commute not accessible by bus or rail. With this type of authoritarianism, it's not hard to imagine that eventually all your movements will be tracked and traced.

What I am saying might sound unthinkable, but the groundwork is already being laid. Various European countries are experimenting with different forms of what they are calling environmentally friendly 15-minute cities.[15] And California already offers an income tax credit to households that don't own cars. It may be hard to swallow, but that's what the future holds.

On another front, more and more global leaders see corporate profits as leverage for getting companies to comply with environmental restrictions. The Swiss MP also said that policies are needed to change the rules of the game so that sustainability becomes the "easier" choice. He praised President Biden's suggestion that governments should do business only with companies that commit to the Paris Agreement, an international treaty on climate change.

Is this the right direction for the world to be heading? Or are these "solutions" a strategy to centralize power and control under the guise of deflecting an environmental apocalypse?

Protecting the planet isn't the only goal on the WEF's agenda. In January of 2023, the WEF published a global risk report based on a survey of 1,200 risk experts, policymakers, and industry leaders worldwide.[16] Each was asked to identify the top risks the globe will likely face that year. Their bleak report, like other recent ones, depicted a grim future. According to their assessment, the next decade will be characterized by environmental and societal crises driven by geopolitical and economic trends. When asked to rate the severity of the items listed, respondents viewed the failure to mitigate climate change as the top risk of the decade.

But when it came to the principal threat of the year, most ranked the cost-of-living crisis as number one—money overtook weather.

> We have seen the return of older risks, inflation, cost of living, trade wars, capital outflows from emerging markets, widespread social unrest, geo-political confrontation, and the specter of nuclear war.[17]

The shift of focus from climate to the economy should grab our attention, especially in light of end-times prophecies regarding a global economy. It is an ominous indicator of where globalists will focus their efforts—implementing a unified approach to the world's economies as a way to avert a monetary collapse.

One of the more perplexing developments is the welcome that China continues to receive from World Economic Forum members.[18] We must remember that China is one of the guiltiest parties regarding pollution and contributing to carbon emissions,[19] which the WEF is in a frenzy to reduce. Let's also not forget China's horrific human rights record. International organizations such as Human Rights Watch continue to document China's abuses, including the imprisonment and torture of more than one million Uyghur Muslims. To quote a 2021 article from Human Rights Watch, "Crimes against humanity are considered among the gravest human rights abuses under international law."[20] Additionally, China's leaders are perpetually threatening the invasion of Taiwan, and if the United States, or any other nation, attempts to stop them, they've promised swift ramifications.

Yet China is allowed a global platform. Why? Many believe that China looks like the answer to much of the world's economic troubles. While reporting on the WEF, Breitbart News reporter John Hayward noted, "Every international organization knows it must tiptoe very carefully around the Chinese Communist Party's short temper and urge for secrecy, or else the Chinese government will completely stop cooperating with even the most urgent endeavors."[21]

The world is looking the other way in its dance with China. We've become addicted to its low-cost, low-quality products—forget about the human cost involved in their production. Why aren't we holding China accountable for its actions? I believe China is being viewed through a foggy haze of self-inflicted, self-serving economic deception.

How does this play into the overall deception of the last days? China's politics and influence have ebbed and flowed throughout history. Still, most Bible scholars believe that China and other nations will make up the kings of the East referred to in Revelation 16:12. China must and will remain a prominent player on the world stage.

From its onset, the World Economic Forum has presented a sunny version of a utopian world, until now. The current view is that we have entered a phase of "permacrisis"—a world buckling under a never-ending cascade of calamities, including war, the climate, rising energy costs, inflation, epidemics, political instability, and worsening economic inequity.[22] This so-called permacrisis seems to be threatening the WEF's model for the future. The worry is that globalism is under siege. But do not be deceived. This is an ancient deception. Consider the words of Chinese military strategist Sun Tzu, written somewhere between 771–256 BC:

> All warfare is based on deception. Hence, when able to attack, we must seem unable; when using our forces, we must seem inactive; when we are near, we must make the enemy believe we are far away; when far away, we must make him believe we are near. Hold out baits to entice the enemy. Feign disorder and crush him.[23]

I believe the first sentence says it all about the select few maneuvering for control. What I find interesting is that Klaus Schwab has been reported to have a god complex.[24] It seems that, like a monarch or pope, he plans to hold on to his power until the end. Little do he and his devotees know how puny their power is compared to a leader coming on the horizon.

The Bible says he is a man who will deceive the deceivers, usurping their authority—but that is for the next chapter.

WE KNOW WHO PREVAILS IN THE END

Appearances can be deceiving, as US Confederate general Stonewall Jackson proved during America's Civil War. The Valley Campaign of 1862 should have ended differently for Stonewall Jackson. While on his way to help defend the city of Richmond, Jackson found himself sandwiched between both halves of the Union army. His 17,000-man force wasn't exactly small, but it was no match for the 52,000 Union soldiers descending upon Virginia's Shenandoah Valley. Trapped in the middle, Jackson pulled off an epic bluff.

> Because of the Lord Jesus Christ, we know how the story ends— He will prevail!

Jackson sent infiltrators behind enemy lines and had them spread the rumor that his forces numbered in the six digits. As Union soldiers closed in from both sides, Jackson marched his army back and forth across the valley, fighting and routing the opposition.

The Union army came to believe the whole area was swarming with Confederate forces—never knowing Jackson was bouncing his men back and forth across the valley. Had the Union generals known of Jackson's small numbers, they would have conducted their campaign differently and crushed his forces. Instead, they withdrew and fled, only to find Jackson waiting in front of them at their garrison at Fort Royal. While General Banks was running away from Jackson to resupply, Jackson got on a train, sneaked around Banks's troops, joined up with additional forces, and captured Banks's garrison.

Stonewall Jackson's deception worked. President Lincoln eventually ordered a full-scale retreat from the area, believing that Jackson's massive army was simply too overwhelming to be defeated.

Likewise, today's small group of global elites wants us to believe they are vast and invincible, so we should give in to their agendas. But we need to keep in mind that Stonewall Jackson's Valley Campaign should have ended differently for the Confederate forces. Had the Union army possessed accurate information, they could have used it to their advantage and routed Jackson. Herein is a lesson for us: We must use what we know to be true to engage those perpetrating half-truths and outright lies.

Two forces pitted against one another—one fighting for freedom, the other bondage—describes the battle for control of our world. Alarming? Overwhelming at times? Yes, on both counts. A massive wave of deception is indeed flooding our world, but you do not need to worry. This need not trouble nor consume you. The very God who presides with a watchful eye over all is the same God who has told us, "In the world you will have tribulation; but be of good cheer, I have overcome the world" (John 16:33).

Because of the Lord Jesus Christ, we know how the story ends—He will prevail!

CHAPTER 10

DAZED BY THE ULTIMATE DECEIVER

C arefully curated four-word headlines, 30-second sound bites, and constant push notifications have lulled us into believing that we understand what is happening in our world. In truth, we know only what the writers or producers of such content want us to know. This steady diet of select bits of information as opposed to knowledge based on a careful examination of facts has contributed to the daze surrounding the critical issues of our day. It has set the stage for the rise of the ultimate deceiver—the Antichrist.

Throughout millennia, wild claims have been made about the future and the Antichrist specifically, and people have believed them. But only the God of the Bible, who exists outside of time and space, can accurately predict events with exactness. The fact that He wants us to know what the future holds should cause us to pay careful attention because, for us living right now, that future could come sooner than we think.

THE WORLD IS READY

Why the sudden sense of urgency? Regardless of their political or religious affiliation, people are angry and frustrated with their leaders. The absence of leadership, global or otherwise, has left nations in turmoil.

In the book of Judges, we are told that when Israel had no king—no leadership whatsoever—every man did what was right in his own eyes (Judges 17:6). This is the nature of fallen man. Leaderless people will take the reins and make do. It isn't until they realize that they are in over their heads that they are driven in desperation and fear to seek a deliverer.

Today, the world is hungry for direction and guidance. I cannot prove my next statements, nor do I want to sound sensational. But I believe that the world is on the brink of the time during which it will see the Antichrist arise. I would not be surprised if he were alive and the hour of his arrival imminent. Jesus warned the disciples about this day and age in Luke 21:28-31 when He said,

> Now when these things begin to happen, look up and lift up your heads, because your redemption draws near. Then He spoke to them a parable: "Look at the fig tree, and all the trees. When they are already budding, you see and know for yourselves that summer is now near. So you also, when you see these things happening, know that the kingdom of God is near."

I live in an area where the summers feel about nine months long. Eventually, spring rains come, and a faint covering of green begins to appear on the ground, creating an anticipation for what comes next. I know that a glorious, velvety green will arrive almost overnight. This serves as a reminder that when I see the slightest hint of end-time prophecy coming into play in our world, I should lift my head and look up because our redemption is near.

Christians might say, somewhat justifiably, "Why do we need to know about the Antichrist? The Bible assures us that we are never going to see him." The number one reason is that he's in the Bible—both the Old and New Testaments. Number two is that you can use this knowledge to warn people about what is coming. Life is going to get intense before the Antichrist arrives, which will make many people receptive to the truth. And number three, you will be able to detect the deceptive spirit of antichrist, which is already in the world (1 John 4:3).

WHO IS THE ANTICHRIST?

There are more than 100 passages of Scripture that refer to the person of the Antichrist, and many more that provide background information. A thorough study of the Antichrist would be extensive, so we are going to limit ourselves to an aerial view of what the Bible says concerning him. This will be a big-picture view, but one that will enable you to pick him out from fellow imposters.

For many, an almost cartoonish image comes to mind when they hear the word *antichrist*. Please don't let the false ideas that he swears using Jesus' name, wears black, and has an upside-down cross emblazoned on his shirt somehow define him. These caricatures couldn't be further from the truth. The term *antichrist* comes from the Greek word *antichristos*, meaning he is against Christ. He is a replacement Christ, an imposter Messiah capable of deceiving the world into believing he is the one they've been waiting for all along.

What sets the Antichrist apart from all other imposters? Second Thessalonians 2:1 is a good starting place for the answer to that question. But before we go further, I want to digress for a moment and give you two facts about the books of 1 and 2 Thessalonians. In 1 Thessalonians, Paul dealt with the characteristics of the church and its rapture, or the gathering together of believers to meet Christ in the air (see 1 Thessalonians 4:16-17). Second Thessalonians was written about a year and a half later, and Paul wrote regarding the events of the second coming and the revelation of the Antichrist during the tribulation period. For our purposes, we'll look at 2 Thessalonians 2:1-10 to give us an initial glimpse of the ultimate deceiver.

Now, brethren, concerning the coming of our Lord Jesus Christ and our gathering together to Him, we ask you, not to be soon shaken in mind or troubled, either by spirit or by word or by letter, as if from us, as though the day of Christ had come. Let no one deceive you by any means; for that Day will not come unless the falling away comes first, and the man of sin is revealed, the son of perdition, who opposes and exalts himself above all that is called God or that is worshiped, so that he sits as God in the temple of God, showing himself that he is God.

Do you not remember that when I was still with you I told you these things? And now you know what is restraining, that he may be revealed in his own time. For the mystery of lawlessness is already at work; only He who now restrains will do so until He is taken out of the way. And then the lawless one will be revealed, whom the Lord will consume with the breath of His mouth and destroy with the brightness of His coming. The coming of the lawless one is according to the working of Satan, with all power, signs, and lying wonders, and with all unrighteous deception among those who perish, because they did not receive the love of the truth, that they might be saved.

What you just read is attention-grabbing, thrilling, and frightening. All of this is rolled together into one powerful portion of Scripture. It is a bit unnerving to consider that the mystery of lawlessness is already at work, and only He who restrains—a reference to the Holy Spirit—is holding the power and deeds of the Antichrist back. One day, the church's mission on Earth will be complete. The church will be raptured, and the Spirit will step aside. For the believer, this future event should create anticipation. But to those who don't know the Lord, Paul's words should act as an urgent warning about the coming leader whom the world will fawn over.

THE SPIRIT OF ANTICHRIST
...Is Ancient

You don't need to be a Christian to have heard about the Antichrist. Mention the number 666, and most people know it is associated with Satan or the Antichrist, and they're curious. They want to know more. Yet believers, who usually have greater knowledge than unbelievers, often act as if the Antichrist were irrelevant to their lives. Satan loves that kind of mentality because it fails to recognize the scope of his influence.

Satan knows Bible prophecy to some extent but doesn't possess any details beyond what is stated in Scripture, which presents a problem for him. With regard to the Antichrist, God has not revealed His timeline. This requires Satan to have an antichrist on hand for each generation. He must always have an antichrist waiting in the wings and the spirit of antichrist operational in preparation for the revealing of "the son of perdition." How far back does this go? All the way to Genesis.

> Cush begot Nimrod; he began to be a mighty one on the earth. He was a mighty hunter before the LORD; therefore it is said, "Like Nimrod the mighty hunter before the LORD." And the beginning of his kingdom was Babel, Erech, Accad, and Calneh, in the land of Shinar. From that land he went to Assyria and built Nineveh, Rehoboth Ir, Calah, and Resen between Nineveh and Calah (that is the principal city) (Genesis 10:8-12).

The significance of this passage is the birth of Nimrod and the introduction of Babylon (Babel). In describing Nimrod, the passage says he was "before the LORD," which means facing or against the Lord. Based on the Hebrew sentence structure, many Jewish scholars believe this means Nimrod was a hunter of men's souls in competition with God. Genesis chapter 11 tells us that Nimrod united people under himself, which sounds innocent enough, except that his motive was to replace God's plan with his own. Bottom line: Nimrod aligned himself against God. He was the first—a prototype—of men led by the spirit of antichrist.

Concerning the name or term *Babylon*, its meaning is broad in scope. It refers to both a city and a system of false religion (see Isaiah 13–14; Revelation 17:5). All cultic and occultic beliefs and practices can be traced back to the ancient Babylonian worship system.

The spirit of antichrist that first appeared in the Old Testament carries through to the end of the New. First John 2:22-23 identifies those who have this same spirit:

> Who is a liar but he who denies that Jesus is the Christ? He is antichrist who denies the Father and the Son. Whoever denies the Son does not have the Father either; he who acknowledges the Son has the Father also.

And in 1 John 4:3, we read,

> Every spirit that does not confess that Jesus Christ has come in the flesh is not of God. And this is the spirit of the Antichrist, which you have heard was coming, and is now already in the world.

Calling someone a liar and antichrist is a strong statement that incorporates the members of every cult we can name. But, perhaps you, like me, have friends who believe in the Father but don't believe in the Son. This is heartbreaking because we don't want to see them end up in a Christless, eternal hell. We want them in heaven with us. But you cannot have the Father without the Son, and you cannot have the Son without the Father. Believing anything less than Jesus' confession "I and My Father are one" (John 10:30) is the spirit of antichrist.

...Will Be Physically Manifested

The spirit that has long been present will one day be manifested. I draw your attention to the definite article "the" in front of the title "Antichrist" in 1 John 4:3. What has been a spirit will become a reality. Satan will possess a living, breathing man. When you and I think of Satan possessing a human, we tend to think of demon possession, but that isn't what will happen with the Antichrist. Satan himself will come inside this man, just as he entered Judas in the upper room while Jesus was celebrating the Passover meal with the disciples (Luke 22:3).

The Antichrist won't operate alone. Satan will provide him with a religious sidekick and assistant. The Bible refers to him as the false prophet, but in modern terms, he's the epitome of a public relations man. He will go where the Antichrist goes and perform miracles designed to exalt him (see Revelation 13:11-13; 16:13; 19:20).

It is important to remember that Satan cannot create anything original. He can only copy and pervert what God has established. Between Satan, the Antichrist, and the false prophet, there will exist an unholy trinity. Satan will pretend to be like the Father, the Antichrist will imitate the Son, and the false prophet will pretend to be like the Holy Spirit. Their combined efforts will have only one purpose: to take their captive adherents straight to hell.

THE ANTICHRIST WILL BE THE CONSUMMATE POLITICIAN
He Will Be a Political Powerhouse

Everything about the Antichrist's thinking and actions will be satanically engineered. He will have characteristics that sway the United Nations, impress the European Union, and outmaneuver the United States. He will be a political superstar, hailed as the man of the hour, and the world will embrace him with what I believe will be a zeal and fervor never before seen.

The Antichrist's rise to fame will happen very quickly, and the Bible says he'll do it through intrigue. If that sounds sinister, it's because it is. He will backstab and lie his way to the number one position among world leaders (see Daniel 8:9, 25; 11:21 for remarkable details).

Not only will the Antichrist come on the scene almost overnight, but he will also have the power to persuade with words. We've seen this type of meteoric rise to fame in charismatic speakers who are able to draw big crowds.

You may have seen old black-and-white newsreel clips of Adolf Hitler ranting and raving like a madman, but those scenes don't show what happened beforehand. Hitler would stand in front of thousands of people without uttering a word for upwards of 20 minutes or so. It's hard to imagine, but crowds waited patiently in prolonged silence until he was ready to speak. Hitler used every bit of his persona and persuasive rhetoric to his advantage, just as the Antichrist will.

More recently, no one had heard of a guy named Barack Obama until the obscure senatorial candidate's keynote speech at the 2004 Democratic National Convention. The political world was captivated by Obama's speech, and he shot to instant fame. The rest is history.

I am not connecting either of these men to the Antichrist, but neither would have risen to power so quickly without charisma and smooth words. The false messiah will have both characteristics in excess, and he will also have something else: the perfect hook—a peace treaty.

He Will Broker Peace in the Middle East

Trends come and go with such regularity that it's hard to keep up. The phrase *trending now* is familiar to many people, and all of us keep up with trends of one kind or another. But do you know the direction the world is trending in the biblical sense? Joel 3:1-2 tells us where we are, and what we can expect next:

> Behold, in those days and at that time,
> when I bring back the captives of Judah and Jerusalem,
> I will also gather all nations,
> and bring them down to the Valley of Jehoshaphat;
> and I will enter into judgment with them there
> on account of My people, My heritage Israel,
> whom they have scattered among the nations;
> they have also divided up My land.

You and I live in the time and space following the fulfillment of God's promise to return the Israelite captives back to Jerusalem and His promise to gather all nations into the Valley of Jehosphaphat. The captives of Judah and Jerusalem are back in the land of Israel, but the gathering of the nations for judgment is yet future. God will judge the nations because of their repeated efforts to divide up His land. Isn't that what politicians have advocated for decades? How often have you heard, "If Israel would give up some land, there will finally be peace in the Middle East"? Dividing up Israel's land might seem a reasonable solution, but if you listen to Israel's enemies, it is clear they will not be satisfied until the nation no longer exists. This is one reason why peace in the Middle East is elusive.

> The Bible's prophetic accuracy should astound even the most stubborn doubter.

The book of Daniel, written nearly 2,500 years ago, says peace in the Middle East, specifically Israel, will be a focal point among world leaders in the last days. I find this fact amazing. Daniel didn't say the United States, Uruguay, Switzerland, or Spain. He said Israel, the nation that wasn't a nation for nearly 2,000 years but suddenly became a nation once again in these last days. The Bible's prophetic accuracy should astound even the most stubborn doubter.

In recent years, there have been a few attempts at peace plans and accords between Israel and its hostile neighbors. An American president has always been a part of the process, but America's involvement may be a thing of the past. The Antichrist will go beyond promising—he will deliver what nearly every American president has attempted since 1948. He will secure peace between Israel and its angry neighbors. How will he do it? Daniel 8:25 says, "Through his policy also he shall cause craft to prosper in his hand; and he shall magnify himself in his heart, and by peace shall destroy many" (KJV).

The Hebrew word for "craft" translates to our English word *deceit* or *intrigue.* Usually people are destroyed by war, but the Antichrist will deceive and destroy by using peace! He will use his ability to broker peace to lull, even daze, the world into a false sense of safety and security.

Daniel 9:27 tells us the peace treaty will be for seven years, but without the Prince of Peace, there can be no lasting peace. Ezekiel chapters 38 and 39 inform us that the Antichrist's treaty won't last. The world's honeymoon of living in Satan's strategically engineered peace will end when the Antichrist breaks the agreement halfway through the seven years.

He Will Bring Prosperity

The Bible indicates that the Antichrist will usher in a new world order that leads to global economic prosperity. Perhaps you've heard the story of King Midas and how everything he touched turned to gold. It is not a far stretch to say that golden is how people will perceive the innovations the Antichrist puts into place. Think about it: Today's industrialized nations are accustomed to the highest standard of living in all of history. Yet, their economies are struggling under the problems created by diminishing workforces, massive debts, and government mismanagement. How will people respond to a leader whose policies lower prices, create jobs, and provide economic security worldwide? They will welcome him with open arms because the world has been waiting for such a man. As the first president of the United Nations General Assembly and former Belgian prime minister Paul-Henri Spaak said in 1957,

> We do not want another committee. We have too many already. What we want is a man of sufficient stature to hold the allegiance of all people and to lift us out of the economic morass into which we are sinking. Send us such a man, and be he a god or devil, we will receive him.[1]

The Antichrist will have brilliant solutions to complex economic problems, one of which involves a cashless society. In the last days, knowledge will increase exponentially (see Daniel 12:4). Now apply that increase to information technology and digital currency. Given the current evidence, we can safely say that the Antichrist will use cashless transactions and digital currency to his full advantage.

Cashless transactions have been around for decades, but most people didn't see the endless possibilities until the COVID lockdowns. Suddenly, life's necessities and luxuries were being bought with a click. It's so easy and time-saving. Everything is tracked, everything is monitored, and everything is safe. Sounds benign, right? Except the Bible tells us what this leads to: "He causes all, both small and great, rich and poor, free and slave, to receive a mark on their right hand or on their foreheads" (Revelation 13:16). The Antichrist will implement some type of electronic biometric identification system or personal authenticator. In fact, there are efforts currently underway to digitalize the entire human body.[2]

There will be those who resist, and the Antichrist will need to make this mark palatable. No doubt he'll mount a multifaceted media campaign showcasing how the mark promotes equality among all peoples and nations and supports global prosperity. And the bonus is that it will curtail social problems.

Human trafficking and the illegal drug trade have thus far evaded law enforcement efforts to shut them down. What is the solution? Go after the money sources. Do you want to dry up the black market for illegal drug transactions? And stop women and children from being traded like commodities? To eradicate those activities will require monetary transparency. In other words, people will need to relinquish some of their personal privacy, but it will be for the common good.

Taking the mark will become easy and the socially acceptable thing to do. People will line up in droves. There was a time when this would have seemed improbable, but no longer. At All Things Digital's 2013 D 11 Conference, Regina Dugan of Google's Advanced Technology and Projects Group made the case that innovation can answer problems that everyone has every day, one of which is the authentication of your identity. One of the options she proposed is a wearable like the electronic tattoo she

displayed on her forearm. Another was an ingestible taken as a daily vita-
min, which she held up for attendees. The pill, already approved by the
Food and Drug Administration for medical purposes, contained a chip
with a switch that, when digested, allowed the whole body to become
an authentication token. Dugan likened it to a superpower that could
allow her to authenticate her identity by simply touching a device such
as a cell phone or computer.[3] But more recently, it is Swedish citizens
who have realized the potential of electronic identification.

> In Sweden, thousands have had microchips inserted into
> their hands. The chips are designed to speed up users' daily
> routines and make their lives more convenient—accessing
> their homes, offices and gyms is as easy as swiping their hands
> against digital readers.
>
> So many Swedes are lining up to get the microchips that the
> country's main chipping company says it can't keep up with
> the number of requests.[4]

People around the world are becoming acclimated to the idea of using
an identifying mark for their personal lives and business dealings. We
all have numbers like those used for banking and Social Security connected to us. The Antichrist could say something like, "Going forward,
you can keep your existing numbers. You'll just simply need to add my
prefix so you can log into our system and be recognized as being on our
team." People will want to be on what is perceived to be the right side,
and they'll say, "Sign me up," except for tribulation saints—believers
who come to faith in Christ during the tribulation period.

I want to make it clear that tribulation saints are not part of the
church. The church—which includes you and me—will have been raptured and will be in heaven prior to the unveiling of the Antichrist. Those
who become saved during the tribulation will die for their faith in Jesus
Christ. "Then I saw the souls of those who had been beheaded for their
witness to Jesus and for the word of God, who had not worshiped the

beast or his image, and had not received his mark on their foreheads or on their hands" (Revelation 20:4).

Those living during the tribulation will need spiritual discernment of the highest order, according to Revelation 13:18: "Here is wisdom. Let him who has understanding calculate the number of the beast, for it is the number of a man: His number is 666." Scripture tells us the Antichrist's system will allow people to choose one of two options: Take the mark as a sign of loyalty and go about life as you wish. Or refuse the mark and be cut off from society, which may cost you your life.

If you are reading this but you're not a follower of Christ, perhaps you're thinking, *When the day comes for that to happen, I would die rather than take the mark.* Let me ask you: If you cannot live for Christ now, how will you die for Him then?

THE ANTICHRIST WILL BE THE ULTIMATE DECEIVER

Unifying the world's religions under the banner of a false religion is a necessary component of the Antichrist's agenda. Secularists argue that religion is the problem, so why unify religious people? Because doing so leaves no one out. All, whether secular or sacred, will work together to bring about the Antichrist's global domination. Imagine the benefit of unifying all religions from the Antichrist's standpoint—complete command, control, and compliance!

If you have an artificial intelligence device like Alexa, ask it what the chief religions of Europe are. Alexa will tell you, "The largest religion in Europe is Christianity, but irreligion and practical secularism are strong." The reason for focusing on Europe here is because the Bible points to a revived Roman Empire as the area from which the Antichrist will arise (see Daniel 2:41-43; 9:26).

There are Europeans who claim to be Christian, but Christianity is on life support and nearly dead on the continent. Yes, Europeans are spiritual people, but ever since the European Union's (EU) creation, many of their municipal events, coinage, flags, and banners have openly celebrated their pagan roots. Even the architecture of the EU's parliament building in Strasbourg, France, bears a striking resemblance to Pieter Brueghel's medieval rendering of the Tower of Babel!

> Deception obscures, and at the same time infiltrates, what Satan has desired from the beginning—to usurp the worship that belongs to God alone.

There are direct ties between Europe's pagan history and the ancient Babylonian system of worship that began with Nimrod. According to Babylonian beliefs, Nimrod's wife, Semiramis, had a son, Tammuz, who was killed. Semiramis prayed to the gods of the underworld for his release from purgatory. Her lamentation lasted 40 days and was called Lent. Through her intercession, Tammuz was raised from the dead, and Semiramis won herself the title of the Queen of Heaven.

If you want to study this further, I encourage you to read *The Two Babylons* by the Reverend Alexander Hislop. The information you will discover may be shocking—it's certainly disturbing—but it cannot be denied.

I want to remind you that there are only two forms of religious worship. One is based on the religiosity of liturgical practices and salvation by works. The other is a humble approach to God, acknowledging, "I cannot save myself. I come to You, Jesus, to save me from my sins." The first is mechanical, the second relational, and herein lies a grave danger: the melding of the two together.

The Antichrist's unified church will be an unholy marriage of Babylonism to the church. Revelation 17:5 calls her "mystery, Babylon the great, the mother of harlots and of the abominations of the earth."

This Babylon is called a whore because she is easily accessible—all roads lead to her—but the foundation of her harlotry isn't of a physical nature. It is religious fornication and adultery, which God says is allegiance to someone other than Him. Her deception lies in the fact that she takes on a cultural form. And she is incredibly dangerous because the souls of many are in her hands. I believe a paganized global church will one day become the accepted religious system endorsed by the global community. It is this woman who will "ride the beast," according to Revelation 17:3.

IT IS ABOUT WORSHIP

Secular or sacred, it all comes down to worship. From the natives in the darkest jungles of the Amazon to those in the Arctic Circle, every culture has practiced some form of worship. Deception obscures, and at the same time infiltrates, what Satan has desired from the beginning— to usurp the worship that belongs to God alone. Isaiah tells us about this in the Old Testament:

> You have said in your heart:
> "I will ascend into heaven,
> I will exalt my throne above the stars of God;
> I will also sit on the mount of the congregation
> On the farthest sides of the north;
> I will ascend above the heights of the clouds,
> I will be like the Most High" (Isaiah 14:13-14).

And Satan's craving for worship resurfaces in the New Testament:

> The devil took Him [Jesus] up on an exceedingly high moun-
> tain, and showed Him all the kingdoms of the world and
> their glory. And he said to Him, "All these things I will give
> You if You will fall down and worship me" (Matthew 4:8-9).

> The son of perdition…opposes and exalts himself above all
> that is called God or that is worshiped, so that he sits as
> God in the temple of God, showing himself that he is God
> (2 Thessalonians 2:3-4).

The Antichrist will use anything and everything within his power to entice people to worship him. You and I have no real idea of what that will look like or mean. If we were exposed to the level of deception that this man will put forth, we would take it—hook, line, and sinker—if it weren't for the Holy Spirit, who dwells within every true, born-again child of God.

Thankfully, we will never see the Antichrist, but that doesn't mean we don't need to safeguard our worship. It is all about worship when it comes to Satan, and when it comes to God, it, too, is all about worship. How, then, can we ensure we are pure, healthy worshippers of God? I leave you with a few simple suggestions.

Get into your Bible daily, and then get up and walk in the Spirit, which is to obey Him. Jesus told the Samaritan woman, "The hour is coming, and now is, when the true worshipers will worship the Father in spirit and truth; for the Father is seeking such to worship Him" (John 4:23).

Be careful not to make worship legalistic. You don't need to follow a liturgical protocol, be inside a church, or wait until Sunday. You can worship God at home, on your way to work, or while walking in the park. Praise Him as a child would—freely with wonder and delight.

Pursue holiness. Your outward appearance is not an indicator of inward holiness, but your reverence for God is. Let the way you live reflect devotion to Him. "Give unto the LORD the glory due to His name; worship the LORD in the beauty of holiness" (Psalm 29:2).

Be passionate. Our English word *enthusiastic* is based on three Greek components. *En* means indwelling or internal, *thus or theos* is God, and *astic* is where we get the words *spasm, movement,* or *action.* When God indwells a person, the result is action. "Serve the LORD with gladness; come before His presence with singing" (Psalm 100:2).

Give expressively. King David said, "I will not offer burnt offerings to the Lord my God with that which costs me nothing" (see 2 Samuel 24:24). Give of your money; give of your time and talents; give of your life.

Love deeply. "You shall love the LORD your God with all your heart, with all your soul, and with all your strength" (Deuteronomy 6:5).

Humans are prone to worship, so the question isn't, "Am I a worshipper?" The question is, "Who, what, and how am I worshipping?" This is where you'll find the battle. Our responsibility is to acknowledge and understand the war being waged against our soul—the place where decisions are made. All the deceptions outlined in this book require a decision—accept or reject, yield or resist, allow or deny. Those decisions come down to one fundamental question: To whom will I bow my knee? I cannot answer it for you, and you cannot answer it for me. Each of us must answer it alone before a holy and righteous God.

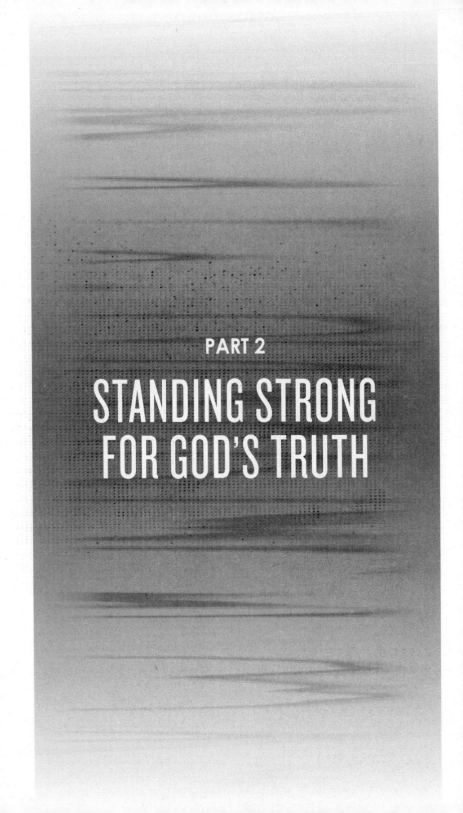

PART 2

STANDING STRONG FOR GOD'S TRUTH

CHAPTER 11

EQUIPPED FOR LIVING IN THE LAST DAYS—PART I

I believe you will agree with me when I say today's world is foreign to us in many ways. It is apparent that there will be no going back to what we once knew as normal. There are many reasons I can give for this conclusion, but we need to look no further than what has become the long-term consequences of the coronavirus pandemic.

When governments used this exaggerated threat to their full advantage, they introduced us to a radically altered world, changing the way we live, and doing so under the banner of public safety.

Today, people are less social, more preoccupied with themselves, angry, violent, lawless, and tragically, more prone to suicide. I see people, including Christians, either drawing closer to God or moving further away from Him. But the most surprising outcome has been unbridled fear. And yes, I am being deliberate in choosing the word *unbridled* to describe the fear that continues to grip our culture and the world today.

When we think of the term *unbridled*, we often relate it to lust and passion, and rightfully so, because the word is often used to describe what is profoundly graphic or gripping to the psyche. In like manner, fear has powerfully seized control of people's hearts and minds worldwide. Fear now drives policies and protocols that affect even the simplest things in our daily lives. It has also caused people to turn on one another. A persistent fear of the unknown has caused such a state of hopelessness that suicide has skyrocketed. All of this points to a world that has come unhinged. It's no wonder people are so scared.

There may be ample reasons for the world to be fearful, but not for Christians. When Jesus talked to the disciples about the last days, He gave them advance warning about the unprecedented deception we have looked at thus far. We now see that the days Jesus spoke of are here. Pervasive deception has led people to surrender to distorted versions of reality on so many fronts. We are locked in an all-out battle over truth.

If you are like me, and I hope you are, my faith always increases when I read about the epic battles of the Old Testament. From one battle to another the combatants may be different, but two facts are always the same: God calls His people to courage, and He equips them to stand and fight.

God has given us the equipment. Now the question is, Will we succumb to fear, or will we, in faith, fight? I believe we are called to fight! And Scripture tells us how we are to do that.

GET DRESSED

The Lord does not expect us to engage the dark forces invading our culture without knowing the specifications and capabilities of our weaponry. In 2 Corinthians 10:4-5, the apostle Paul tells us that "the weapons of our warfare are not carnal but mighty in God for pulling down strongholds, casting down arguments and every high thing that exalts itself against the knowledge of God." Paul goes into greater detail regarding our spiritual armament in Ephesians 6:10-18. Let's look at the passage, and then explore how it applies to us.

Finally, my brethren, be strong in the Lord and in the power of His might. Put on the whole armor of God, that you may be able to stand against the wiles of the devil. For we do not wrestle against flesh and blood, but against principalities, against powers, against the rulers of the darkness of this age, against spiritual hosts of wickedness in the heavenly places. Therefore take up the whole armor of God, that you may be able to withstand in the evil day, and having done all, to stand.

Stand therefore, having girded your waist with truth, having put on the breastplate of righteousness, and having shod your feet with the preparation of the gospel of peace; above all, taking the shield of faith with which you will be able to quench all the fiery darts of the wicked one. And take the helmet of salvation, and the sword of the Spirit, which is the word of God; praying always with all prayer and supplication in the Spirit, being watchful to this end with all perseverance and supplication for all the saints (Ephesians 6:10-18).

Paul begins with, "Finally, my brethren." These words to the Ephesian church are meant for us too. The word "finally" means from this point forward. This exhortation has powerful implications for each of us. It doesn't matter what happened yesterday. Forget about it and leave it behind, and from this moment on, go forward suited up with the whole armor of God.

It is incredible how the Bible speaks to us in the twenty-first century using imagery from the past that spurs our imagination: kingdoms, armor, swords, shields, and breastplates. God describes the believer's armor in a way most of us would say sounds medieval and dangerous, yet the Holy Spirit inspired specific words that are timeless in their application. Even today, we understand very clearly the details of our spiritual armament.

We are urged to wear the whole armor so that every vital part of us is covered and ready for life's battles. Have you ever heard the term *armed to the teeth*? It brings to mind old swashbuckler-type movies in which the main character is getting ready to fight, and he's making sure he has everything he needs. Perhaps he has a couple of swords strapped to his back, pistols holstered on his thighs, and a knife or two on each calf. And then he realizes, "Hey, my mouth is free. If I clench it between my teeth, I can carry one more weapon—a dagger." That's what it means to be fully equipped, ready for whatever comes our way. That is how we as Christians need to approach life.

Once armed, we have incredible strength and power. "Finally, my brethren, be strong in the Lord and in the power of His might." I love this! Notice that Paul is not talking about my strength and might or yours, but God's strength and His might. These are guaranteed to us because by putting on God's armor, we are putting on Christ.

Romans 13:12-14 connects "arming up" with "putting on Christ" in this way: "The night is far spent, the day is at hand. Therefore let us cast off the works of darkness, and let us put on the armor of light. Let us walk properly, as in the day, not in revelry and drunkenness, not in lewdness and lust, not in strife and envy. But put on the Lord Jesus Christ, and make no provision for the flesh, to fulfill its lusts."

The realization that "the night is far spent, the day is at hand" should excite us. But if this causes you to become stressed and worried, look at it this way: You live in a unique time in history. Maybe you're enrolled in college or you have a job and a family. Perhaps you're involved in serving at church. All that is great. Keep at those things. But at the same time, Romans 13:12-14 makes it clear what manner of people we ought to be as we go about our lives.

Don't be deceived into thinking that you can put on Christ and keep wearing the fleshly garments of your old life. You must have an internal resolve to discard those tattered rags. If you are engaging in habits or attitudes that make you stumble, let them go. The only way to avoid being tripped up and sidelined is by becoming intimately acquainted with God's truths and commands. When you know what the Bible says and arm yourself with it, you will be dressed and ready for battle.

GET WISE
The Enemy's Identity

Simply put, modern life is demanding. It's easy to forget that we are fighting an enemy unlike any other entity—it is not human. And it's hard, if not impossible, to fight someone you aren't aware of or don't believe exists.

Tragically, polls tell us that a significant number of professing Christians deny the existence of Satan. Some say he is a fairy-tale figure or that he is only a personification of evil. As J. Dwight Pentecost said, "We hear very little today about Satan, and consequently, many who recognize Satan's existence and acknowledge that he is the enemy of their souls are ill-prepared to meet him."[1] Sadly, if that is true of you, he has you right where he wants you.

In discussing this world's situation and the devil's involvement in it, author C.S. Lewis brilliantly pointed out, "Enemy-occupied territory— that is what this world is." Lewis went on to say,

> Christianity is the story of how the rightful king has landed, you might say landed in disguise, and is calling us all to take part in a great campaign of sabotage. When you go to church you are really listening-in to the secret wireless from our friends: that is why the enemy is so anxious to prevent us from going. He does it by playing on our conceit and laziness and intellectual snobbery. I know someone will ask me, "Do you really mean, at this time of day, to re-introduce our old friend the devil—hoofs and horns and all?"

> Well, what the time of day has to do with it I do not know. And I am not particular about the hoofs and horns. But in other respects my answer is "Yes, I do." I do not claim to know anything about his personal appearance. If anybody really wants to know him better, I would say to that person, "Don't worry. If you really want to, you will. Whether you'll like it when you do is another question."[2]

The Enemy's Methods

Satan's ability to hide his intentions and activities is why Ephesians 6:11-12 exhorts us, "Put on the whole armor of God, that you may be able to stand against the wiles of the devil. For we do not wrestle against flesh and blood, but against principalities, against powers, against the rulers of the darkness of this age, against spiritual hosts of wickedness in the heavenly places." You cannot detect or deflect the wiles of the devil without your armor on.

In Ephesians 6:11, the Greek word translated "wiles" is *methodeia*, from which we get our English word *methodology*. Isn't that interesting? The devil has methods, just like human military leaders do, such as the legendary strategist Genghis Khan.

Genghis Khan was known for equipping his armies with the best weaponry possible, but if a weapon or strategy underperformed in battle, Khan would adapt by simply inventing something new to meet the challenge. Here is a sampling of his tactical methods: the Wearing-Down Tactic, Confuse and Intimidate Tactic, Lightning and Surprise Attack Tactic, Open-Ended Tactic, and the Hot Pursuit Tactic.[3] It should be no surprise that Khan's tactics bear a distinct resemblance to Satan's methodology against God's people.

Satan can and will throw everything at us, including the proverbial kitchen sink. But take heart—God, in His goodness, has made us tougher in Him than we may realize. How do I know? Through Peter's example.

In Luke 22, we find Jesus seated with His disciples. They were enjoying their last meal together when Jesus turned to Simon Peter and told him something that probably made the disciple's blood run cold: "Simon, Simon! Indeed, Satan has asked for you, that he may sift you as wheat" (verse 31).

Now that statement may not seem all that bad to us because unless you are a farmer, you don't harvest or process wheat. You just walk through the bakery aisle at the supermarket, pick out your favorite brand of bread, pay for it, and go on your way. You might not understand the sifting process, but Peter did.

In those days, wheat had to be threshed and winnowed before a small amount was put into the center of a bowl-like sieve. A worker would then vigorously shake the sieve to separate the grain from the chaff, or what was edible from what wasn't. Sifting was a necessary step in sorting out usable grain.

We can only guess at the rest of Jesus and Peter's conversation with that imagery uppermost in Peter's mind. It may have gone something like this:

> Jesus: "Peter, Satan has asked for you. He has asked to beat you up."
>
> Peter: "Yeah, it's okay. No big deal because You told him no, right? Right? I mean, wow, that was a close call."
>
> Jesus: "Actually, Peter, I didn't tell him no. When he is done with you—and you will survive—you are to use that experience to strengthen your fellow believers."

Satan's goal was to break Peter, yet we know from church history that Satan's sifting did quite the opposite. Satan meant to destroy Peter, but God used the situation to make him a spiritual giant. Wise, mature, battle-hardened Peter took every bit of what he learned through that experience and shared it with others. I encourage you to read the book of 2 Peter and see the results for yourself. You will be blessed by Peter's insights for your Christian walk.

Does the prospect of facing what appears to be overwhelming opposition have you cowering in fear? It shouldn't, and the biblical account of an incident involving the prophet Elisha and his servant explains why.

In 2 Kings 6, beginning in verse 14, we read about an exchange that took place between this man of God and his servant. While Elisha was sound asleep, the servant woke up and saw that they were completely surrounded by Syria's massive military force, which was ready to destroy

Israel. These were scary-looking people—a dirty, fierce fighting machine! The servant responded by saying, in essence, "It's over. We're going to die."

Elisha woke up and uttered a statement that should comfort the heart of every child of God: "Do not fear, for those who are with us are more than those who are with them" (verse 16). Elisha's servant could physically see the enemy soldiers, but he couldn't see what mattered most.

Faith sees what fear cannot.

Here's what happened next: "Elisha prayed, and said, 'Lord, I pray, open his eyes that he may see.' Then the Lord opened the eyes of the young man, and he saw. And behold, the mountain was full of horses and chariots of fire all around Elisha" (verse 17).

Can you imagine? Elisha prays, the servant blinks, then opens his eyes to see an enormous host of heavenly forces—or angelic creatures—positioned to destroy the invading Syrian army arrayed against God's people.

The horses and chariots of fire were real. Faith sees what fear cannot. The next time circumstances shout at you to give up because there is no way out, ask God to open your eyes.

GET STRONG
Set a Line of Defense

There have been plenty of books written on spiritual warfare, but the classic I reach for is William Gurnall's *The Christian in Complete Armour*. The value of his insights will blow your mind. His wisdom is that good. If you are prone to buying books, this is the one to get! In the meantime, I want you to consider this pointed question from Gurnall and its relationship to how we are to prepare, in advance, to fight the good fight of faith: "What have we Bibles for, ministers and preaching for, if we mean not to furnish ourselves by them with armour for the evil day?"[4]

In Ephesians 6:13, Paul alerts us to the need for a good defense: "Therefore take up the whole armor of God, that you may be able to withstand in the evil day, and having done all, to stand." A key reason God has given you a suit of spiritual armor is so that "you may be able to withstand."

Your first line of defense in holding back enemy forces comes from putting up a wall of protection against that which is opposing you. That wall is designed to deflect attacks.

Recent veterans of urban warfare in the Middle East will nod in agreement with the necessity of walls because they have inadvertently become experts in concrete, as in concrete barriers. Barriers placed in strategic locations provide invaluable security and protection against attack. Troops even give these barriers nicknames like Jersey, Alaska, and Texas, based on their size. But regardless of their size, these barriers provided safety in enemy territory.

The amount of time you put into safeguarding your life and your spouse and your family with a wall built using the Word of God will determine your level of safety during these dangerous times. Since coming to Christ more than four decades ago, I've instituted a simple method of countering spiritual attacks. When I feel the enemy pressing in and I want to guard against fear, doubt, or anxiety, I print out Bible verses. Then I put them up in strategic places around the house—on the mirror where I shave, above the kitchen sink, on the windowsill near where I study. I'll even tape them to my car dashboard. Reading and rereading these reminders of the power of God and what He has promised to do for His people serves as a concrete barrier between me and my adversary.

Stand Firm

Next, we are told to stand firm: "Stand therefore, having girded your waist with truth" (Ephesians 6:14). The concept of girding your waist has to do with using a belt.

Some of the illustrations you see of ancient Roman soldiers wearing a belt show a simple, thin leather strap around the waist, but that doesn't accurately depict what the soldiers actually wore or what Paul had in mind when he wrote this description. These belts were large enough and thick enough to connect with the warrior's breastplate and hold his various implements of warfare, including his scabbard and sword, keeping them close at hand and ready. Strips of leather also hung from the front of the belt to protect the lower body. So these belts were strong and substantial!

> Girding ourselves firmly with God's truth is essential, for it determines whether you and I will stand or fall.

Biblically girding yourself tightly with God's truth enables you to stand firm, immovable, and to protect your vital organs. If I compare the belt to a girdle, women instantly understand what I am talking about. But another way to illustrate this is through an injury I received when I was younger.

One evening when I arrived home from work, I got out of the car, bent down to lift the handle on the garage door, and as I did so, I immediately saw stars. I fell to the ground, moaning in agony. I felt like I was going to die, so my wife and I made a trip to the emergency room that night.

A doctor diagnosed that I had a herniated disk. To help relieve the pain, he wrapped me up so tight that I felt as if my waist had shrunk five or six inches. I could hardly breathe. Every other part of my body was free to move around, but the wrap around my waist was so firm it kept me upright. That is precisely what Paul had in mind when he wrote about the belt of truth.

Girding ourselves firmly with God's truth is essential, for it determines whether you and I will stand or fall.

Peter helps to broaden our understanding of what it means to be girded when he says, "Gird up the loins [the deep inward parts of your heart and soul] of your mind" (1 Peter 1:13). The literal translation of the Greek text here refers to preparing your mind for action. The idea is that of a man gathering the folds of his long garment and tucking the garment into his belt so that he can move about unhindered.

You and I cannot afford to allow our thoughts to aimlessly flap in the breeze and risk losing our enthusiasm for the things of God and our effectiveness as Christians. In the battle for truth, the opposition is subtle in its attempts to sway our thinking. Be wise regarding who you are listening to and what you are reading. Gird your mind with unadulterated, pure biblical doctrine so that you don't become loose and lackadaisical concerning spiritual things. As Hebrews 2:1 says, "We must give the more earnest heed to the things we have heard, lest we drift away."

What's beautiful about truth is that you don't need to create it. God's eternal truth stands—strong, steady, and unchanging. So much of what is said, posted, and printed these days is reported as truth but isn't. This naturally leads us to ask: What is truth, and what are the benefits of knowing the truth? According to Webster's 1828 dictionary, truth is "conformity to fact or reality; exact accordance with that which is or has been or shall be. The truth of history constitutes its whole value. We rely on the truth of the scriptural prophecies."[5]

But perhaps the best answer comes from a 2,000-year-old conversation. On the day of his arrest, trial, and crucifixion, Jesus appeared before Pontius Pilate, the governor of Judea. After hearing Jesus speak regarding His kingdom and followers, Pilate famously asked, "Are you a king then?"

Jesus answered and went beyond Pilate's question by saying, "You say rightly that I am a king. For this cause I was born, and for this cause I have come into the world, that I should bear witness to the truth. Everyone who is of the truth hears My voice."

Pilate pressed Jesus further by asking, "What is truth?" (John 18:37-38). This exchange between Pilate and Jesus is relevant to every thinking person. If we stop and consider its ramifications, it should cause us to sit up, take notice, and make a personal decision regarding truth.

Standing before Pilate was Jesus Christ, the Son of God, who claimed to be the truth of God incarnate. This was no veiled or secret revelation that Jesus made of Himself. To those who were looking for the Messiah, the Old Testament scriptures gave exacting proofs that He was who He said He was (John 5:39). And, who but God could predict the manner of His death and resurrection? "They will mock Him, and scourge Him, and spit on Him, and kill Him. And the third day He will rise again" (Mark 10:34). This same Jesus said, "I am the resurrection and the life. He who believes in Me, though he may die, he shall live" (John 11:25).

You can debate the sincerity of Pilate's questions. Was he merely doing his duty in questioning Jesus? Or did he genuinely believe that Jesus held the answers he was searching for? Either way, what is not in question is that truth leads to satisfaction when encountered, embraced, and walked in.

It is God's desire that each of us would walk in the truth. The idea of walking in the truth is both beautiful and practical. We are all familiar with walking; it comes very naturally to us. You may not think of this very often, but the moment you are unable to walk, you lose your freedom. Not having the ability to walk steals from you the opportunity to explore or to be independent. It reduces your entire world to a geographical location, sometimes limiting you to a chair or bed.

But, if you can walk freely, then the world is before you, and nothing is off limits. Once again, I love the practicality of the Bible. When you walk in the truth of God's Word, it illuminates everything around you that is shadowy and distorted. "Your word is a lamp to my feet and a light to my path" (Psalm 119:105). You are to hold up the truth like a lantern and walk in its light. But to do so, you must assimilate it into your life.

The entire Bible lays down truths we should know—line upon line, precept upon precept. Our responsibility is to follow the example of the Berean believers in Acts 17:11. They searched the Scriptures daily to determine whether the teachings they were hearing lined up with Old Testament prophecies and doctrines. And for that there is no substitute but to consume the Bible on a regular basis and determine to put it into practice.

GET ENGAGED

As the days grow darker and more evil, I cannot reiterate this strongly enough: I believe that God has been preparing His church and is calling us to a new level of even greater commitment. He has appointed each of us to be alive at this moment in time. We should be waking up every morning with anticipation and excitement at the thought of what He has in store for us. I like how the Puritans viewed the church and their Christian faith. It will sound radical to some ears, but it's biblical.

The Puritans believed that there were two aspects to the church: the church militant and the church triumphant. The church militant engages the world, battles wickedness, and proclaims the gospel while shining the light and love and truth of Christ to a dark world. Church history is full of examples of men and women who wholeheartedly believed that they should engage their culture by taking a strong stand—believers like William Wilberforce, Samuel Adams, and William Carey.

The name William Wilberforce had largely been forgotten until its reintroduction to our generation through author Eric Metaxas's *Amazing Grace*. As a member of the English Parliament, Wilberforce understood what it meant to have influence. But following his acceptance of Christ, his life took on a new purpose: using his position to affect change. "My walk is a public one," he wrote in his diary. "My business is in the world, and I must mix in the assemblies of men or quit the post which Providence seems to have assigned me."

Wilberforce became an ardent abolitionist. He campaigned tirelessly for 45 years to abolish slavery—many times standing alone in this pursuit. In an infamous speech to Parliament regarding the facts of the slave trade, Wilberforce closed with, "Having heard all this, you may choose to look the other way, but you can never again say that you did not know." That speech changed history. He witnessed the slave trade's abolishment at age 47, but it wasn't until he was on his deathbed 30 years later that he learned of the final passage of the Slavery Abolition Act, allowing 700,000 slaves in the United Kingdom to be set free.

William Wilberforce's efforts spurred on a group of abolitionists in the United States—men of tremendous influence: Dr. Benjamin Rush, the first surgeon general; John Adams, the second president; and the ringleader, whose name may surprise you: Thomas Jefferson.

The church militant is here on Earth, but the church triumphant is yet to come. We will have our ultimate triumph when we stand before the Lord, rejoicing in heaven. But the fact that we're not there yet means we need to stand strong—to build a line of defense so that we can persevere. Now is not the time to give up.

Knowing that this day would come, Jesus prayed to His Father for us, "They are not of the world, just as I am not of the world. Sanctify them by Your truth. Your word is truth. As You sent Me into the world, I also have sent them into the world. And for their sakes I sanctify Myself, that they also may be sanctified by the truth" (John 17:16-19). The word "sent" implies equipment for a definite mission. We can go forth with great courage because of the magnitude of support that truth provides. In front, behind, and flanking us like an impregnable wall, the power of heaven itself is with us.

To be an effective believer today is as it has always been—it is to understand the deployment orders that have come to us from our King. He has commissioned us to go into this world of hostile arguments, sinister agendas, and demonic doctrines.

The Bible tells us that the eyes of the Lord are looking "to and fro throughout the whole earth, to show Himself strong on behalf of those whose heart is loyal to Him" (2 Chronicles 16:9). He is looking for men and women who refuse to look the other way and will not back down in fear. I believe they are here among us. I believe you are one of them.

In 2 Corinthians 6:7, Paul wrote that as we serve God, we are to do so "by the word of truth, by the power of God, by the armor of righteousness on the right hand and on the left."

This is how we engage. This is how we stand. This is how we fight.

CHAPTER 12

EQUIPPED FOR LIVING IN THE LAST DAYS—PART 2

All is fair in love and war, or so the world believes, and when countries go to war, they use whatever means necessary to win. Take, for example, this almost comical but highly effective bit of trickery carried out by the Allied Forces during World War 2.

> The Ghost Army had one goal: Deceive Hitler's forces and their allies...
>
> Credited with fine-tuning the ancient art of deceptive warfare, the American military units of the Ghost Army used inflatable tanks and trucks to cloak the true size and location of U.S. forces. They played ear-piercingly loud recorded sounds to mimic troop movement. They sent out misleading radio communications to scramble German intelligence...
>
> The Germans fell for the ruse.[1]

If the idea that a war machine like Nazi Germany could fall for such a scheme seems far-fetched, remember that we live in an age that has turned its back on logic and reason, and fallen for pseudoscientific beliefs in place of real science. In the battle for truth, you and I are being conditioned—groomed, if you will—to embrace lies even when the truth is right in front of us.

In light of this, I believe that every Christian needs to be able to answer these two questions: How can I protect myself? And, Where do I go from here?

In the previous chapter, we looked at some of the pieces of the Christian's armament as Paul described them in Ephesians 6:10-18. I ended with the belt of truth, and in this chapter, we'll continue to look at how God has equipped us to stand strong against our adversary, the devil. But before we move on, I want to share a couple of my go-to verses. I turn to these passages when I get the wind knocked out of me, spiritually speaking, or when I need to refocus, and they certainly apply to the times in which we live.

The first is Jeremiah 29:11-13, especially verse 12, which guarantees that the Lord listens when I call upon Him in prayer, and that when I search for Him wholeheartedly, I will find Him.

> I know the thoughts that I think toward you, says the LORD, thoughts of peace and not of evil, to give you a future and a hope. Then you will call upon Me and go and pray to Me, and I will listen to you. And you will seek Me and find Me, when you search for Me with all your heart.

The second is God's encouragement to Joshua:

> No man shall be able to stand before you all the days of your life; as I was with Moses, so I will be with you. I will not leave you nor forsake you. Be strong and of good courage, for to this people you shall divide as an inheritance the land which I swore to their fathers to give them. Only be strong and very courageous, that you may observe to do according

to all the law which Moses My servant commanded you; do not turn from it to the right hand or to the left, that you may prosper wherever you go (Joshua 1:5-7).

Joshua was quite a man. He was a spy, faithful assistant to Moses, called by God to lead Israel into the Promised Land, and was just like us. We know he was like us because, throughout the book of Joshua, God speaks to him and says, "Don't be afraid" and "Be of good courage." Joshua was called to do great things, but he was fearful and sometimes lacked courage.

You may feel just like Joshua: inadequate, weak, or fearful. That's okay. But don't stay that way. I urge you to find out where your strength lies. Arm yourself with the whole armor of God. With that in mind, let's read Ephesians 6:10-18 and continue with our look at the armor God has given us.

> Finally, my brethren, be strong in the Lord and in the power of His might. Put on the whole armor of God, that you may be able to stand against the wiles of the devil. For we do not wrestle against flesh and blood, but against principalities, against powers, against the rulers of the darkness of this age, against spiritual hosts of wickedness in the heavenly places. Therefore take up the whole armor of God, that you may be able to withstand in the evil day, and having done all, to stand.

> Stand therefore, having girded your waist with truth, having put on the breastplate of righteousness, and having shod your feet with the preparation of the gospel of peace; above all, taking the shield of faith with which you will be able to quench all the fiery darts of the wicked one. And take the helmet of salvation, and the sword of the Spirit, which is the word of God; praying always with all prayer and supplication in the Spirit, being watchful to this end with all perseverance and supplication for all the saints.

BOLD AND READY

The apostle Paul's understanding of how the spiritual world affects our physical world is something that the church needs to grab ahold of today. I know things are coming at us left and right, but we need to stop allowing them to trip us up. We need to get bold and stand our ground. When I say "get bold," I don't mean an arrogant, ugly way like the ungodly do. That type of boldness is brazen, egotistical, and unattractive. But godly boldness comes when you understand what it means to "put on the breastplate of righteousness" (Ephesians 6:14).

You and I have zero righteousness of our own. Let me say that again: zero. If we think that we can create some form of personal righteousness, I guarantee it will be a morality concocted in arrogance. In contrast, when we accept Christ's blood-bought payment for our sins, Jesus turns to us and gives us His righteousness as a breastplate.

I want you to notice that the placement of the breastplate is over the Christian's vitals, which have to do with the things of the spirit. The righteousness of Almighty God covers and protects the spiritual lungs and heart of a born-again believer. Let that sink in for a moment. Let this wonderful and amazing truth settle into your soul. It should cause you to take a deep breath and go about life with absolute confidence and boldness.

I love that God provides us with righteousness because it makes a tremendous difference in how we handle life. We read in Proverbs 28:1, "The wicked flee when no one pursues, but the righteous are bold as a lion." The wicked flee out of fear, falsely believing the world is after them and closing in fast. But the righteous have no such worry. Like the psalmist, we can say, "I will not be afraid. What can man do to me?" (Psalm 56:11).

When Jesus taught the Beatitudes in the Sermon on the Mount, He said, "Blessed are those who are persecuted for righteousness' sake, for theirs is the kingdom of heaven" (Matthew 5:10). If you take a stand against abortion, you will be called hateful. Or, if you speak out against redefining sexuality, you will be labeled narrow-minded and potentially lose your livelihood. It is a fact that "all who desire to live godly in Christ Jesus will suffer persecution" (2 Timothy 3:12), but fear of the repercussions is not a reason to shrink back. Living in the freedom of Christ's righteousness will embolden you to do the right things.

The believer's boldness originates from the readiness that comes from "having shod your feet with the preparation of the gospel of peace" (Ephesians 6:15). Implied here is that you might have shoes on, but the gospel of peace goes on over them for protection wherever your feet carry you throughout your day. Why is this true? Because first and foremost, you are justified by faith and have peace with God through Jesus Christ (Romans 5:1).

As a Christian, you are no longer at war with God. Christ has brought peace between you and Him, which means you are not contending with Him. There is no longer any friction between you. At least, that's true about your *spiritual standing* before God. But perhaps this isn't entirely true about your *everyday relationship* with God. You may be a Christian, but you're constantly arguing and fighting with Him about how things are going in your life. You need to lay those issues down at the foot of the cross and live at peace with Him. How can you give out the peace of the gospel to those who are troubled if you yourself have no peace? You cannot give away what you don't have.

Now, if you are not all that concerned about giving out the gospel, the truth behind having your feet shod will sting, but I say the following in love. The Christian in complete armor, according to Ephesians 6:15, is someone who shares the gospel. If God has transformed your life, you have something to say.

You might protest, "I'm not a preacher." I didn't say you have to be a preacher. You could argue that you're not outgoing or that you don't know enough of the Bible. I'm not saying you need to change your personality or become a Bible scholar. But have you honestly experienced Jesus Christ in your life? If you can answer yes, you can be as blind and deaf as Helen Keller was and still communicate the power of God—which she did.

If the thought of sharing the gospel terrifies you, ask God to open a door of opportunity and see what happens. I am confident that He will bring the right person at the right time—tailor-made just for you. That neighbor, co-worker, or stranger will walk away blessed, and I guarantee, so will you.

Let's be honest: Have you ever eaten a fantastic meal or done something cool and fun and told someone about it? Of course you have. I submit to you that there is a high probability that because God has touched your life, you have something to say to others about what He has done.

It could be that you've never told someone about Jesus. Today is the day to make a change. You have something unique to communicate—I'm talking about your personal testimony. In Luke 8:38, we read about a man Jesus delivered from demon possession who "begged Him that he might be with Him." That sounds like a reasonable request, but Jesus sent him away. Why? Jesus knew what that man needed to do. "Return to your own house, and tell what great things God has done for you" (verse 39). Perhaps God is nudging you, asking, "How about your family?" They are an excellent place to start, but don't stop there! The more you tell your story, the more natural it will become to share it. You will find it easier and easier to witness for Christ.

Be willing to lay aside your excuses and insecurities. God wants to use you for His glory. I can say that with authority because I used to stutter. When I was a kid, I was bullied and made the brunt of jokes. One of my elementary school teachers even singled me out by making me stand on a desk to read a book, leading everyone to laugh at my expense.

I didn't grow out of stuttering as some kids do. When I proposed to Lisa, it seemed like it took forever for me to get the words out: "W-w-will y-you m-m-m-marry me?" Then, in 1983, I was out witnessing with a little group. I was always the one praying in the background, but that night was different. I saw this young woman and felt compelled to talk to her. I didn't hear a voice, but it was as though God had grabbed my shirt. I sensed His power at work. I knew that to resist would be disobedient. So, I walked up to her and said, "Excuse me. Would you mind if I share with you about Jesus Christ?" She said, "No, not at all." At that moment, God healed my tongue. I shared the gospel, and we prayed together. I didn't stutter then, I don't stutter now, and ever since that night, no one has been able to keep me quiet.

Friend, listen. Do you have a problem you're struggling with, as I did? Has "it" become an excuse for not being bold? Let Jesus Christ get ahold of your life and transform you so you can be a vessel of His spiritual power.

CLOSE AND PROTECTED

The next weapon Paul brings to our attention is the shield of faith. He begins Ephesians 6:16 by saying "above all," which tells us our shield should be a top priority because we will need it to quench "the fiery darts of the wicked one." In our modern world, we associate darts with games mounted on the wall, and if you add fire to them, well, that just makes the game more exciting. But the fiery darts of biblical times were altogether different. "Fiery" is from the Greek word *pyros*. It is where we get our English word for *pyrotechnic* or *fireworks*. "Darts" is *belos*, which speaks of missiles. Paul is letting us know that when Satan attacks, he uses major firepower! This is why the shield of faith is essential.

> Your greatest possession…is your faith as it rests in the power and truth of the Bible.

In ancient warfare, soldiers would dip their arrows in tar or pitch, set them ablaze, and launch them at the opposing forces. When a Roman soldier saw such fireballs coming at him, he got down on one knee, put up his shield, and took the hit. But there was a different tactic when a whole unit was advancing in the face of enemy firepower. As the enemy catapulted fiery darts, the commander shouted, "Chelóna, chelóna," which means "turtle." And together, the men held their shields in a way that resembled a tortoise's shell.

The first row of men would crouch down and hold their shields from their shins to their eyes to cover the formation's front. Those in the back would place their shields overhead, overlapping them with the shields of those in front to offer protection above. If the formation were large, those on the sides and rear would face outward, their shields overlapping with those behind, thus protecting the whole group. This is how Christian fellowship should be!

Believer, you are given the shield of faith as a defense against Satan, and I know this may seem like I am exaggerating to make a point, but hear me out. Your greatest possession is not the car in your driveway, your boat, your stock portfolio, or your health. It is your faith as it rests in the power and truth of the Bible.

I have heard the accusation, "Bible, Bible, Bible. That's all you ever talk about." It's true, and for this reason: "Faith comes by hearing, and hearing by the word of God" (Romans 10:17). Every time you read a Scripture verse or hear sound biblical teaching, your faith grows, and your shield gets bigger and bigger and bigger. Trust me. In battle, you want a big shield, which leads me to ask: When your personal struggles are intense with arrows flying from every direction, and your heavenly commander calls out "Turtle," do you have fellow believers you can lock shields with?

If your response is, "I talk to people all week long at work. I'm tired. I don't want to hang out with anyone," I understand. But listen: We're engaged in a spiritual battle of epic proportions—we need to be linked together. I encourage you to ask the people sitting closest to you on Sunday mornings out for breakfast or lunch, or to exchange prayer requests. Really get to know each other. Do whatever it takes to go beyond waving in the parking lot or shaking hands after worship, because "your adversary the devil walks about like a roaring lion, seeking whom he may devour" (1 Peter 5:8).

Depending on where you live, you might call them cougars, panthers, or pumas, but here in Southern California, we call them mountain lions. Regardless of what you call these big cats, they have one thing in common: They're waiting for the one who is all alone. And that is what the devil is waiting for too. He will stalk you, watching you for weeks and months, sometimes years. He'll wait to make his move, and strike when you've stopped fellowshipping with other believers who will build your faith, stand by you, and pray with you in tough times. Satan loves isolated Christians. They're easy prey.

COVERED IN TRUTH

Battle-ready soldiers must be strong-minded warriors, so it is no accident that "the helmet of salvation" (Ephesians 6:17) sits above all the other pieces of our spiritual armament. It is in the region of the mind where Satan's most significant attacks regarding salvation take place.

I have a Kevlar helmet given to me by a Marine Corps colonel who saw numerous deployments in Afghanistan and Iraq. It is unbelievably lightweight and incredibly strong. The helmet is made with layered composites that give soldiers freedom of movement, visibility, and maximum head protection. That Kevlar helmet and its multiple capabilities is a perfect picture of the protection that the helmet of salvation provides.

There is no question that when the helmet is securely placed and well fitted, it defends us against attacks on the doctrine of salvation, known as soteriology. Satan knows that what we believe about salvation affects nearly every area of our lives. Unfortunately, far too many Christians have misunderstood or inadequately learned what salvation entails and how secure their salvation truly is. Here are three basics:

1. The Bible says, "If you confess with your mouth the Lord Jesus and believe in your heart that God has raised Him from the dead, you will be saved" (Romans 10:9).

2. Jesus said, "I give them eternal life, and they shall never

perish; neither shall anyone snatch them out of My hand. My Father, who has given them to Me, is greater than all; and no one is able to snatch them out of My Father's hand" (John 10:28-29).

3. You, dear saint, are eternally saved and wonderfully secure until the day of redemption because you have this promise: "Now He who establishes us with you in Christ and has anointed us is God, who also has sealed us and given us the Spirit in our hearts as a guarantee" (2 Corinthians 1:21-22).

The moment you accept Christ, God sees you as a new creation (2 Corinthians 5:17). He even gives you a new heart, the initial and all-important first step in salvation. But the mind is something altogether different. We are not given a new mind. When the Bible speaks about the mind, it refers to our thought life with its passions, desires, hurts, and the like. This part of us remains under the ongoing sanctifying work of the Holy Spirit and must be renewed daily through the Word (Romans 12:2).

> The God of all creation gave His only Son to reconcile you to Himself and give you eternal life. He will not abandon you now.

Oh, how we need salvation's truths covering our minds when Satan determines to take us down! One of the great heroes in the faith, Charles Spurgeon, suffered severe bouts of depression. He described them as dark and sinister feelings that left him feeling alienated from God. Does it surprise you that a spiritual giant such as Spurgeon faced this kind of struggle? It shouldn't. We all struggle from time to time, even with things like depression and hopelessness. But there is a solution to this problem: Preach the gospel to yourself every day!

Immerse yourself in the scriptures that speak about salvation and the magnitude of God's love for you. Remind yourself of all that is now yours. Counterattack with verses like 2 Samuel 22:2-3: "The LORD is my rock and my fortress and my deliverer; the God of my strength, in whom I will trust; my shield and the horn of my salvation, my stronghold and my refuge; my Savior."

The God of all creation gave His only Son to reconcile you to Himself and give you eternal life. He will not abandon you now. Strap the helmet of salvation firmly in place and set your mind toward eternity. It will fill you with enthusiasm and liberate you to see this world in a Christ-centered way. The knowledge that the same power that raised Christ from the dead is at work in you (Ephesians 1:20) will infuse you with resiliency to face life's ups and downs. You will become a formidable warrior when suited for combat and crowned with the helmet of salvation, able to say, "Yet in all these things we are more than conquerors through Him who loved us" (Romans 8:37).

POWER FROM ON HIGH

We've already seen the strength and protection offered by our spiritual weaponry, so I feel like I'm doing an infomercial when I say, "But wait, there's more." Ephesians 6:17 commands us to take up "the sword [Greek *machaira*] of the Spirit, which is the word of God." Of all the implements provided to the Christian soldier, only the sword is deployed as an offensive weapon. You may have heard the saying, "The best defense is a good offense," and I believe it is even truer when applied to the sword of the Spirit.

The sword most often associated with Roman warriors is the colossal broadsword. But when a battle became intense, and men turned to grapple with one another in hand-to-hand combat, the *machaira*—carried on the hip of every centurion—became the weapon of choice. The *machaira* was small (approximately 14-18 inches long), sharp, and deadly. Soldiers were highly trained in its usage and knew precisely where to thrust the blade. They knew that when they pushed the sword up to its hilt, to the point that it stopped, they would strike a vital organ. The victor was then confident that his opponent was going down for good.

Christian, never forget that your enemy fights to win, even unto death. I know that sounds violent, but the invisible battles mounted against you, your family, and the world around you are fierce, and the enemy is unrelenting. This is the time to make sure that you know how to fight using the sword of the Spirit—the Word of God.

William Gurnall wrote,

> A pilot without his chart, a scholar without his book, and a soldier without his sword are alike ridiculous. But, above all these, it is absurd for one to think of being a Christian without knowledge of the Word of God and some skill to use this weapon.[2]

It is impossible to overstate your need to become skillful in using the sword of the Spirit. We have heard from countless so-called experts who argue against biblical truth in their respective fields of late, and if you listen carefully, you'll hear evidence that they have spent time honing their deceptive arguments. It seems that in every arena of life, what we hear makes good sound evil and evil sound good. I urge you to train yourself to use specific scriptures to counterattack and slay deceptive thoughts and attitudes that lead people away from God's will.

For instance, if you are talking with someone who supports euthanasia for the elderly and infirm, it's ineffective to quote John 14:6, "I am the way, the truth, and the life. No one comes to the Father except through Me." That won't work. It is an excellent verse for evangelism, but not the right one for a conversation about euthanasia. But if you know someone who is struggling in their marriage, encouraging that person with a verse like Ephesians 4:32—"Be kind to one another, tenderhearted, forgiving one another, even as God in Christ forgave you"—works perfectly.

COMMUNICATING WITH THE COMMANDER

Paul has gone to great lengths to help Christians understand the power of their spiritual armor, but it's the final piece—prayer—that, when neglected, renders us weak in our warfare. Ephesians 6:18 commands us to pray "always with all prayer and supplication in the Spirit." Prayer commissions the sword of the Spirit, the breastplate of righteousness, feet prepared with the gospel of peace, the shield of faith, the helmet of salvation, and the belt of truth. Prayer causes all our weaponry to work together.

I have heard people say, "Well, I guess there's nothing left to do but pray," as though prayer is a last-ditch resource when all other efforts have failed. I hope this isn't how you view your access into God's throne room because that is not what the Bible teaches.

> Our constant prayers prepare us for battle and the critical hour of engagement when heaven's support is needed most.

Numerous times in Scripture, we are exhorted to pray without ceasing, which shows us that talking to God ought to be as natural to us as breathing is to our bodies. As fish swim through water and birds fly through air, so would the Lord have you and me as accustomed to and comfortable with prayer. Yet we have fallen prey to the many books, sermons, and conversations in which prayer is made out to be some massive, laborious, complicated act. In so many ways, it has been described as nearly impossible to enter into. I believe Satan desires to get you and me so intimidated that we would rather give up on prayer and walk away, frustrated.

Don't get me wrong. Prayer does require initiative on our part. We are called to maintain a constant line of communication with the Lord, which means prayer doesn't just happen automatically. It takes effort, but it's not hard—it's all about sharing with the Lord the burdens on our hearts and seeking His guidance.

In a word, through prayer, we are constantly in contact with our high command as we are deployed in this world. When we pray, we are immediately connected with all the powers of heaven above. We are granted wisdom, insight, and understanding, and sometimes, God will reveal what is to be the target of our prayers.

On one of my visits to Israel, I was allowed to be an eyewitness to a military mission in which a drone, high overhead, was used to monitor a small group of Israeli commandos working on disabling a known terrorist location. Those electronic eyes looked down upon everything and communicated all that those commandos needed to know to eliminate the danger. Vital information was transmitted in an up-and-down link of conversation. Soldiers in Tel Aviv oversaw the situation, giving directions to those in a distant region—everything worked flawlessly—as though they were standing face to face and speaking to one another. The communication was crystal clear. The observation platform from high above was perfect, allowing a handful of men to take out a powerful, looming threat.

I see our conversations with God as being similar to the Israelis' communications with each other. Through prayer, God allows us to see what otherwise remains invisible to the natural self. And we have that same up-and-down, earth-to-heaven, and heaven-to-earth connection to our Father and the captain of the Lord's host, Jesus Christ.

Our constant prayers prepare us for battle and the critical hour of engagement when heaven's support is needed most. When that hour arrives, we should be driven to our knees to get our marching orders.

COMMISSIONED

Outstanding leadership has always defined the turning points in the history of man—leadership that inspired and encouraged people to move beyond their limitations and abilities. Authors have filled libraries with countless pages of the exploits of the great men and women who shaped their culture and beyond—some, for all time. They responded to a summons loftier and greater than themselves, to live beyond themselves.

I could list the leaders who have shaped the world and brought us to the place where we are today, but even the greatest leaders become irrelevant unless they spawn hope within us. No matter what you think of his politics, Napoleon Bonaparte belonged in that category. In battle and during times of looming defeat, when Napoleon's forces heard that he was on his way, they fought with an extra burst of strength and vigor. The hope that he could soon arrive at any moment led them to perform heroic feats of courage as they advanced with one eye on the battle and the other looking to the horizon for Napoleon's appearance.

If a leader like Napoleon could generate such hopeful zeal, how much more is that true of our Leader—the only true source and foundation of hope—God Almighty, manifested in the person and ministry of Jesus Christ!

Globally, nations, including the United States, are imploding. We are watching our freedoms collapse, and believers now live under an ever-present specter of persecution. Yet amidst opposition and difficulty, Jesus Christ promises a hope that protects our minds and hearts.

We are equipped with everything needed to stand in the face of adversity, but Ephesians 6:18 mandates that we also be "watchful to this end with all perseverance." This is an incredible time of growth for the church collectively and individually—and we need to persevere and allow the difficulties of these days to do their work in us just as 1 Peter 1:3-9 says they will.

> Blessed be the God and Father of our Lord Jesus Christ, who according to His abundant mercy has begotten us again to a living hope through the resurrection of Jesus Christ from the dead, to an inheritance incorruptible and undefiled and that does not fade away, reserved in heaven for you, who are kept by the power of God through faith for salvation ready to be revealed in the last time.

> In this you greatly rejoice, though now for a little while, if need be, you have been grieved by various trials, that the genuineness of your faith, being much more precious than gold that perishes, though it is tested by fire, may be found

to praise, honor, and glory at the revelation of Jesus Christ, whom having not seen you love. Though now you do not see Him, yet believing, you rejoice with joy inexpressible and full of glory, receiving the end of your faith—the salvation of your souls.

We've got our marching orders. They're very direct, clear, liberating, and so joyful that we can't help but be excited at the prospect of what is to come.

Each of the elements of your spiritual armament I've set before you—the belt of truth, the breastplate of righteousness, feet shod with the preparation of the gospel of peace, the shield of faith, the helmet of salvation, and sword of the Spirit—and what they will accomplish should engender a firm and steadfast hope like never before in the history of the church.

I don't mean to sound uncaring or cavalier when I say this, but every day that you and I wake up to something else going wrong in our world should give us cause for increased hope. I understand the temptation to throw your arms up in disgust and quit as you see the scandalous conduct of elected officials, our culture falling apart, and ministries and churches failing to stem the tide. I say to you, "Don't do it!" Your response should be the opposite. Remember, from God's perspective, nothing that is happening is unexpected. He said things would get much worse in the last days as we move along on the prophetic calendar.

The dazed state of the world is a profound warning to work out our salvation with reverence and awe. Time is short. Neither you nor I know when God will call us home, either through the rapture or death. But this we do know: God's Word announces to us that Jesus is coming again—soon.

The hope of Christ's return causes me, in my later years, to look for even more opportunities to minister. Hope causes me to speak up and take a stand against this age that is so very wicked. With one eye on the battle and the other on the horizon looking for Jesus, I have never been more encouraged to stay the course and to advance.

My goal for this book has been to lead you to understand that there is no reason to be sad or hopeless. On the contrary, I pray that you have been encouraged to lay those feelings aside, get up, and make your life matter with a sanctified recklessness for the kingdom of God. As you move forward, may you be the kind of believer who causes hell to sit up and take notice as heaven applauds you and the great cloud of witnesses rejoices over your faithfulness to the Lord Jesus Christ.

NOTES

Chapter 1—The Daze of Global Deception

1. U.S. Department of Transportation Federal Highway Administration, *Road Weather Management Program*, https://ops.fhwa.dot.gov/publications/fhwahop12046/rwm05 _californial.htm.

Chapter 2—Dazed by Spiritual Deceivers

1. James Montgomery Boice, "Galatians," in *The Expositor's Bible Commentary*, vol. 10, gen. ed. Frank E. Gaebelein (Grand Rapids, MI: Zondervan, 1976), 429. Emphasis added.

Chapter 3—Dazed by Deceptive Spirits

1. This term was first applied to Madalyn Murray O'Hair by *Life* magazine in 1964, according to David Van Biema, "Where's Madalyn?," *Time*, February 10, 1997, https://content.time.com/time/subscriber/article/0,33009,985893-2,00.html.

2. *US News & World Report*, January 31, 2000.

3. H. Allen Orr, "Gould on God, Can religion and science be happily reconciled?," *Boston Review*, October 1, 1999, https://www.bostonreview.net/articles/h-allen-orr-gould-god/#:~:text=Gould%27s%20vision%20of%20the%20proper,other%20plenty%20of%20elbow%20room.

Chapter 4—Dazed by Doctrines of Demons

1. Oxford Languages, https://languages.oup.com.

2. Jack Lynch, "Every Man Able to Read" Literacy in America, *Colonial Williamsburg* (CW Journal: Winter 2011).

3. This illustration appeared in a business newsletter I received online, and I saved the illustration. But at the time of this writing, the website content is no longer available, and I am unable to recall the source.

4. C.H. Spurgeon, "A Weighty Charge," sermon preached at the Metropolitan Tabernacle on March 26, 1876, https://www.spurgeongems.org/sermon/chs1286.pdf.

Chapter 5—Dazed by Deceptions Within the Church

1. H.A. Ironside, *Illustrations of Bible Truth* (Chicago, IL: Moody Press, 1945), 62-63.

Chapter 6—Dazed by Easy Believism

1. C.H. Spurgeon, *Lectures to My Students, First Series* (London: Passmore and Alabaster, 1875), 77.

2. C.H. Spurgeon, "The Enemies of the Cross of Christ," sermon preached at the Metropolitan Tabernacle on October 26, 1884, https://www.spurgeon.org/resource-library/sermons/the-enemies-of-the-cross-of-christ/#flipbook/.

Chapter 7—Dazed by the Deceptive Cry for Unity

1. Palwasha L. Kakar and Melissa Nozell, "Pope Francis in the Cradle of Islam: What Might It Bring?," *United States Institute of Peace*, February 19, 2019, https://www.usip .org/publications/2019/02/pope-francis-cradle-islam-what-might-it-bring.

2. AFP, "Pope Calls for Global Unity Ahead of Grand Imam Meeting in Bahrain," *The Guardian*, November 4, 2022, https://guardian.ng/news/world/ pope-calls-for-global-unity-ahead-of-grand-imam-meeting-in-bahrain/.

Chapter 9—Dazed by the Deception of the World

1. Jennifer Graham, "From J.K. Rowling to Josh Hawley, writers with unpopular beliefs are under siege. Now Amazon is on the battlefield," *Desert News*, March 8, 2021, https://www.deseret.com/indepth/2021/3/8/22308119/bill-clinton-helped-create -conservative-publishing-where-headed-josh-hawley-regnery-amazon-google.

2. Ron Charles, "Outcry over book 'censorship' reveals how online retailers choose books—or don't," *Washington Post*, April 22, 2021, https://www.washingtonpost.com/ entertainment/books/outcry-over-book-censorship-reveals-how-online-retailers-choose -books--or-dont/2021/04/21/258d37bc-a1fc-11eb-a7ee-949c574a09ac_story.html.

3. Cecile Ducourtieux, "Roald Dahl reprint reignites criticism against sensitivity readers," *Le Monde*, March 1, 2023, https://www.lemonde.fr/en/culture/article/2023/03/01/ roald-dahl-reprint-reignites-criticism-against-sensitivity-readers_6017847_30.html.

4. Oliver Tearle, "Who said, 'A Lie Is Halfway Round the World Before the Truth Has Got Its Boots On'?," *Interesting Literature*, December 6, 2021, https:// interestingliteraturecom/2021/06lie-halfway-round-world-before-truth-boots-on -quote-origin-meaning/.

5. "Extreme temperatures linked with heart disease deaths," *Harvard T.H. Chan School of Public Health*, December 12, 2022, https://www.hsph.harvard.edu/news/ hsph-in-the-news/extreme-temperatures-linked-with-heart-disease-deaths/.

6. Gabriel Hays, "CNN analyst slammed after writing COVID deaths are being overcounted: 'TWO AND A HALF YEARS LATE,'" *New York Post*, January 14, 2023, https://nypost.com/2023/01/14/dr-leana-wen-writes-that-covid-deaths -are-being-overcounted/.

7. Peter J. Wallison and Benjamin Zycher, "This Winter We Will See the Dangerous Results of Climate Alarmism," *AEI*, December 12, 2022, https://www.aei.org/articles/ this-winter-we-will-see-the-dangerous-results-of-climate-alarmism/.

8. James Taylor, "Climategate 2.0: New E-Mails Rock the Global Warming Debate," *Forbes*, November 23, 2011, https://Forbes.com/sites/james taylor/2011/11/23/ climategate-2-0-new-e-mails-rock-the-global-warming-debate/.

9. AZ Quotes, https://www.azquotes.com/quote/184966.

10. Thomas Barrabi, "Bill Gates claims his private jet habit 'not part of' climate problem," *New York Post*, February 9, 2023, https://nypost.com/2023/02/09/ bill-gates-defends-private-jet-habit-despite-climate-activism/.

11. "Climate change the greatest threat the world has ever faced, UN expert warns," *United Nations Human Rights Office of the High Commissioner*, October 21, 2022, www.ohchr .org/en/press-releases/2022/10climate-change-greatest-threat-world-has-ever-faced-un -expert-warns/.

12. Klaus Schwab, "The Great Reset," *World Economic Forum,* https://www.weforum.org/focus/the-great-reset.

13. Isa Auken, "Welcome To 2030: I Own Nothing, Have No Privacy and Life Has Never Been Better," *Forbes,* November 10, 2016, https://www.forbes.com/sites/worldeconomicforum/2016/11/10/shopping-i-cant-really-remember-what-that-is-or-how-differently-well-live-in-2030/?sh=5fac89173509.

14. Klaus Schwab, *Twitter,* 12:28 a.m., November 13, 2016, https://twitter.com/Davos/status/797717774885863424.

15. Aitor Hernandez-Morales, "Don't lock me in my neighborhood! 15-minute city hysteria sweeps the UK," *Politico,* March 1, 2023, https://www.politico.eu/article/dont-lock-me-neighborhood-15-minute-city-hysteria-uk-oxford/.

16. "Global Risks Report 2023," *World Economic Forum,* January 11, 2023, https://www.weforum.org/reports/global-risks-report-2023/in-full.

17. Bill Pan, "WEF Elites Rate 'Cost-of-Living Crisis' as World's Top Risk in 2 Years," *The Epoch Times,* January 14, 2023, https://www.theepochtimes.com/wef-elites-rate-cost-of-living-crisis-as-worlds-top-risk-in-2-years_4984437.html.

18. Bradford Betz, "World Economic Forum chair Klaus Schwab declares on Chinese state TV: 'China is a model for many nations,'" *Fox News,* https://www.foxnews.com/world/world-economic-forum-chair-klaus-schwab-declares-chinese-state-tv-china-model-many-nations.

19. "Report: China emissions exceed all developed nations combined," *BBC News,* May 7, 2021, https://www.bbc.com/news/world-asia-57018837.

20. "Break Their Lineage, Break Their Roots." *Human Rights Watch,* April 19, 2021, https://www.hrw.org/report/2021/04/19/break-their-lineage-break-their-roots/chinas-crimes-against-humanity-targeting.

21. John Hayward, "Chinese Communists Endorse the Davos Spirit," *Breitbart,* January 16, 2023, https://www.breitbart.com/asia/2023/01/16/chinese-communists-endorse-davos-spirit/.

22. Ishaan Tharoor, "The worry in Davos: Globalization is under siege," *The Washington Post,* January 16, 2023, https://www.msn.com/en-us/news/world/the-worry-in-davos-globalization-is-under-siege/ar-AA16qj7Q.

23. "The Art of War by Sun Tzu: Summary & Notes," *Graham Mann,* https://www.grahammann.net/book-notes/the-art-of-war-sun-tzu.

24. Peter Caddle, "'God Complex': Klaus Schwab Will Run WEF Like A Pope Until Death, Associates Claim," *Breitbart,* January 17, 2023, https://www.breitbart.com/europe/2023/01/17/god-complex-klaus-schwab-will-run-wef-like-a-pope-until-death-associates-claim/.

Chapter 10—Dazed by the Ultimate Deceiver

1. Quoted in David L. Larsen, *Telling the Old Story: The Art of Narrative Preaching* (Grand Rapids, MI: Kregel, 1995), 214.

2. Mohamed Kulay. "Regina Dugan at D11 2013," https://www.youtube.com/watch?v=B1EcocAF8.

3. Regina Dugan, "Regina Dugan at D11 2013," YouTube, 8:54, 2013, https://youtu.be/fzB1EcocAF8.

4. Ahmed Banafa, "Technology Under Your Skin: 3 Challenges of Microchip Implants," *BBA Open Mind*, April 5, 2021, www.bbvaopenmind.com/en/technology/innovation/technology-under-your-skin:-3-challenges-of-microchip-implants.

Chapter 11—Equipped for Living in the Last Days, Part 1

1. J. Dwight Pentecost, *Your Adversary the Devil* (Grand Rapids, MI: Kregel Publications, 1997), 9.

2. C.S. Lewis, *Mere Christianity* (New York: Simon & Schuster, 1996), 51.

3. Gerelee, "Genghis Khan's Military Tactics," *Amicus Mongolian Travel Company*, https://www.amicusmongolia.com/mongolia-military-tactics-genghis-khan.html.

4. William Gurnall, *The Christian in Complete Armour*, vol. 1 (Peabody, MA: Hendrickson Publishers, 2018), 248.

5. Noah Webster, *American Dictionary of the English Language*. S. Converse, 1828.

Chapter 12—Equipped for Living in the Last Days, Part 2

1. Vimal Patel, "Ghost Army, a World War II master of deception, finally wins U.S. recognition," *Pittsburgh Post-Gazette*, February 6, 2022, https://www.pressreader.com/usa/pittsburgh-post-gazette/20220206/281861531911902.

2. William Gurnall, *The Christian in Complete Armour*, vol. 2 (Peabody, MA: Hendrickson Publishers, 2018), 194.

FAST FORWARD
YOUR FAITH.

The Gospel Will
Not Be Censored

The Real Life Network was created to offer censor-free, biblically based content that will strengthen your faith and character through Bible teachings, educational content, and special features.

Free For You To Enjoy
On Any Device

The Real Life Network is available to you for free on your favorite device, anywhere, anytime! Never miss a moment to enrich your life with shows that inspire.

Entertainment For
The Whole Family

The Real Life Network has something for everyone. Choose from a wide range of categories, including culture, current events, faith in government, and kids' programming.

Sign up at
REALLIFENETWORK.COM

To learn more about Harvest House books and
to read sample chapters, visit our website:

www.HarvestHousePublishers.com

HARVEST HOUSE PUBLISHERS
EUGENE, OREGON